Sometimes
the
smallest
things take up
the most room
in your
heart.

Winnie the Pooh

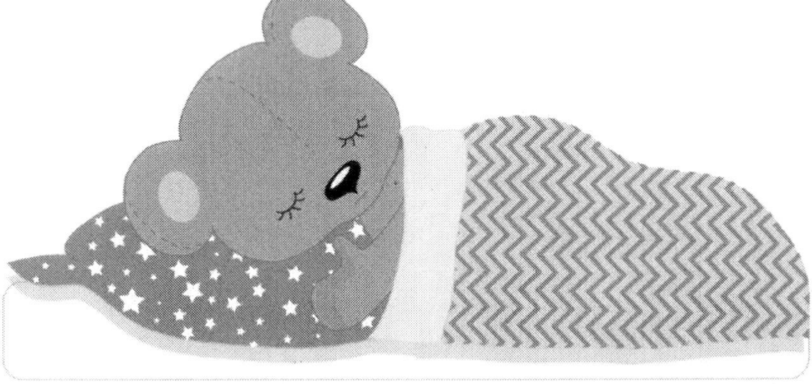

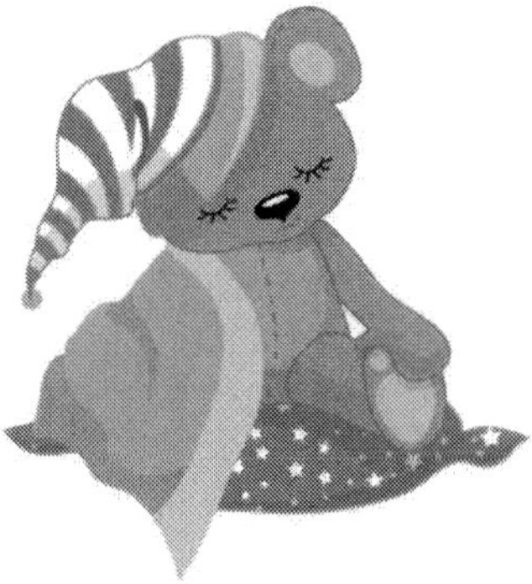

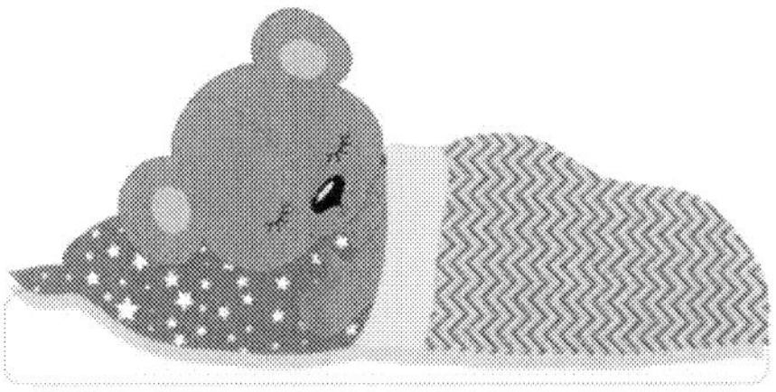

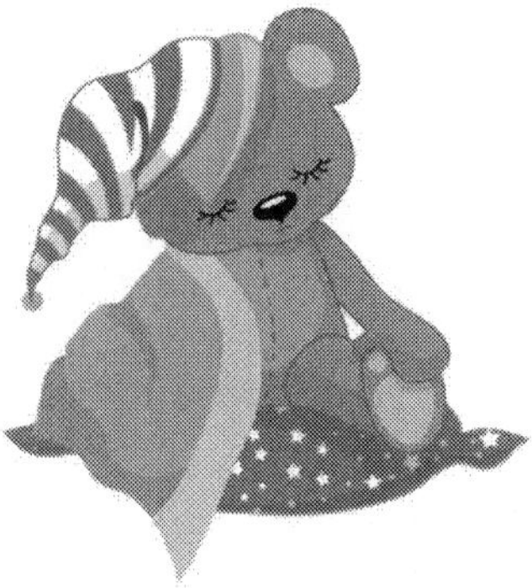

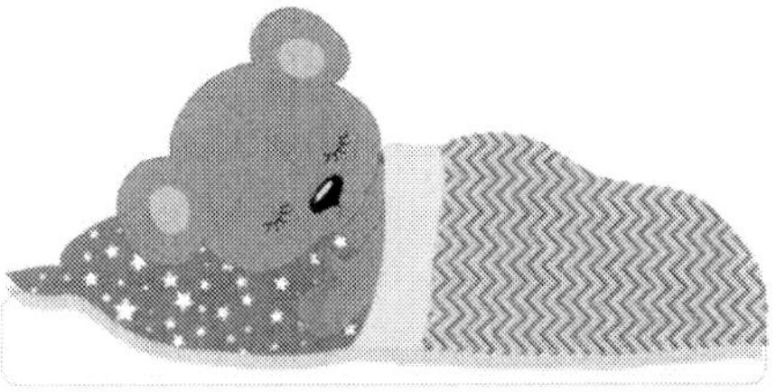

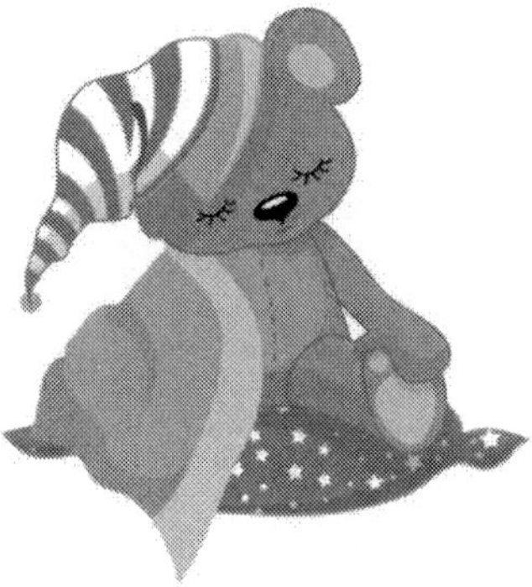

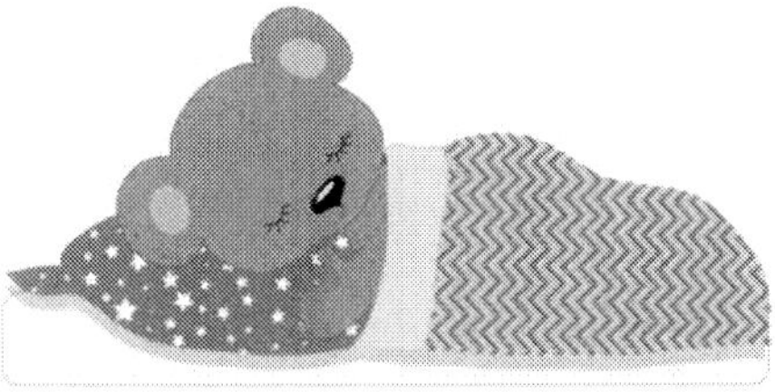

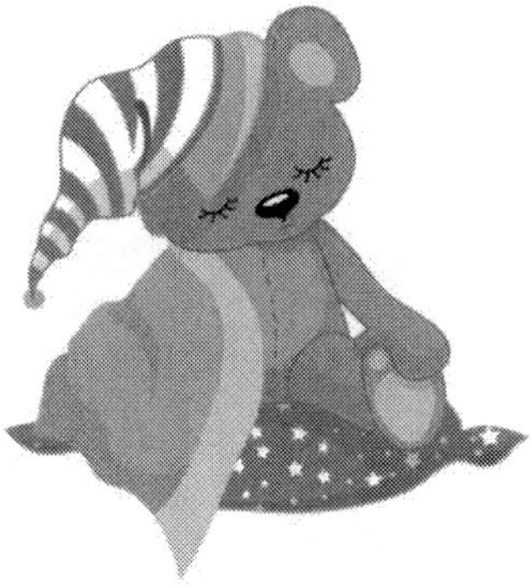

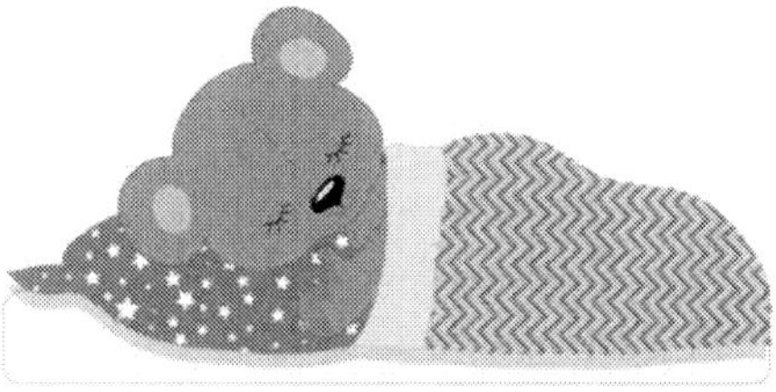

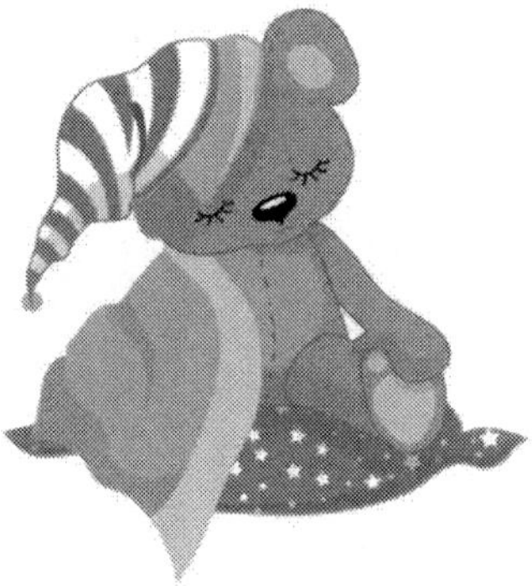

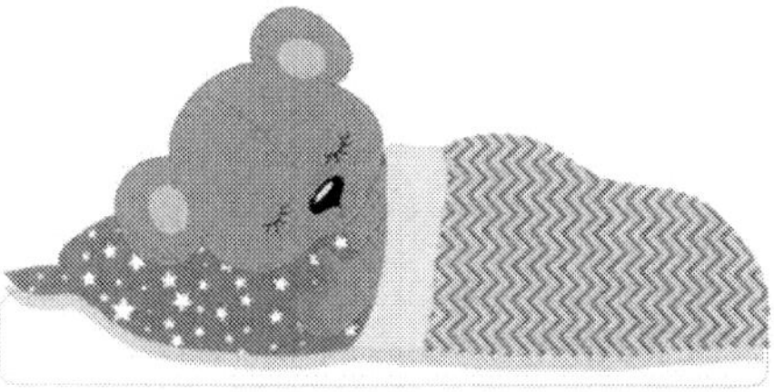

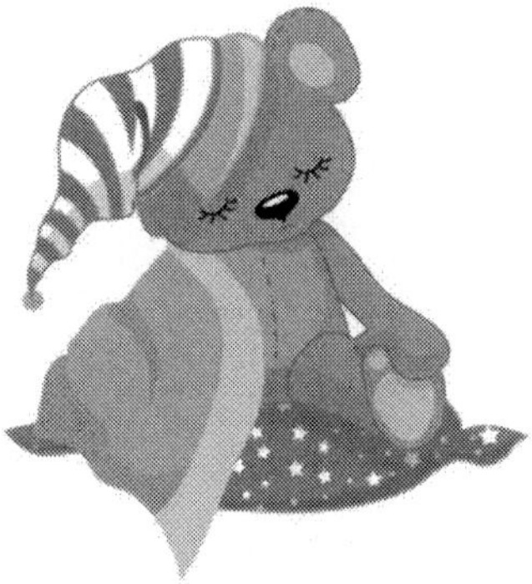

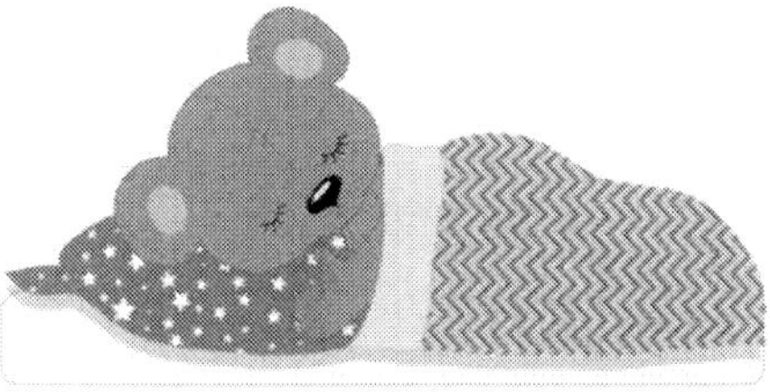

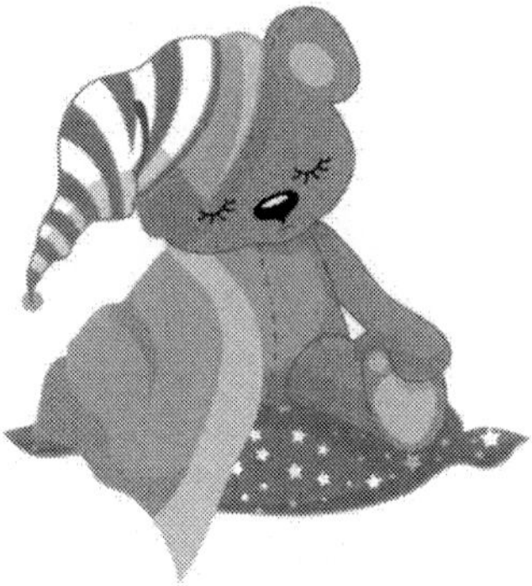

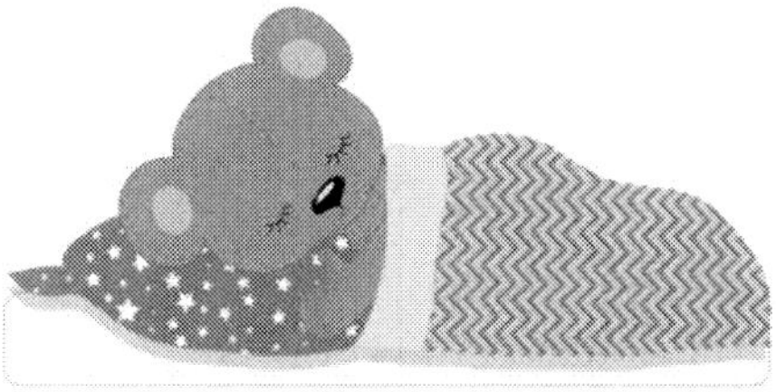

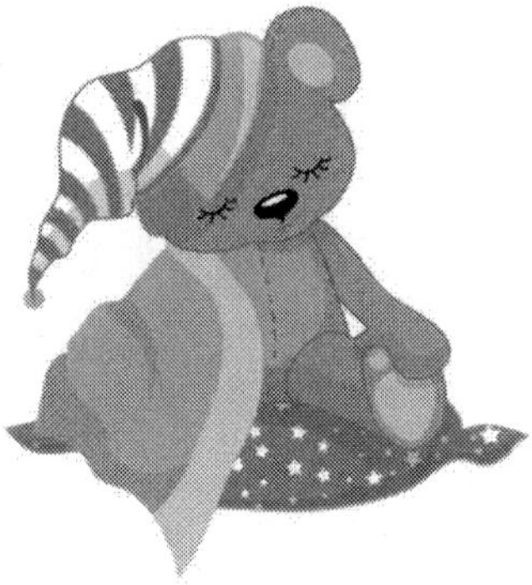

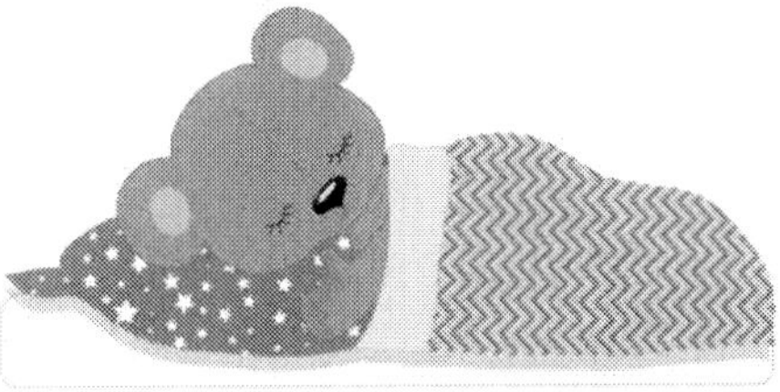

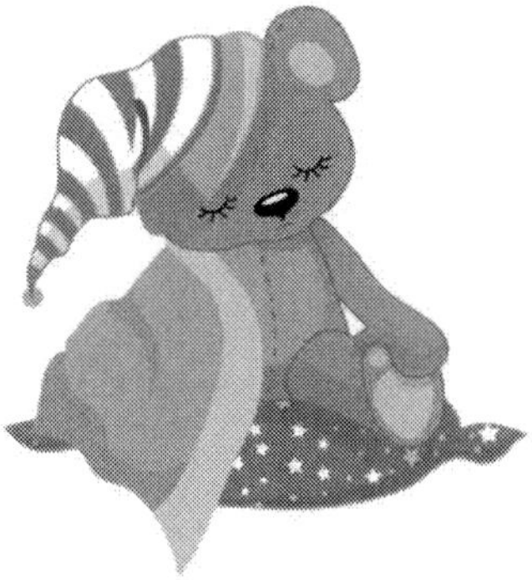

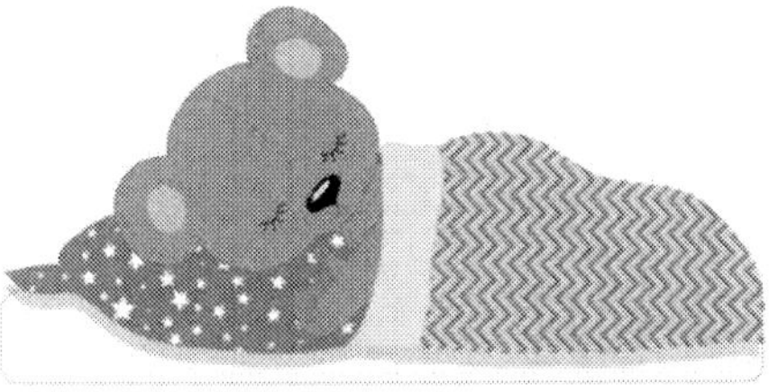

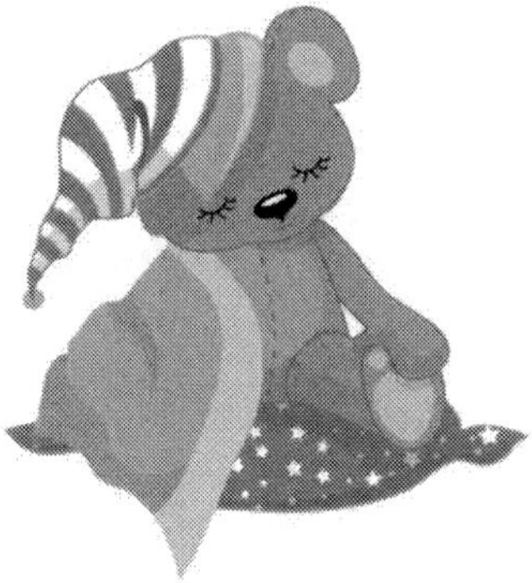

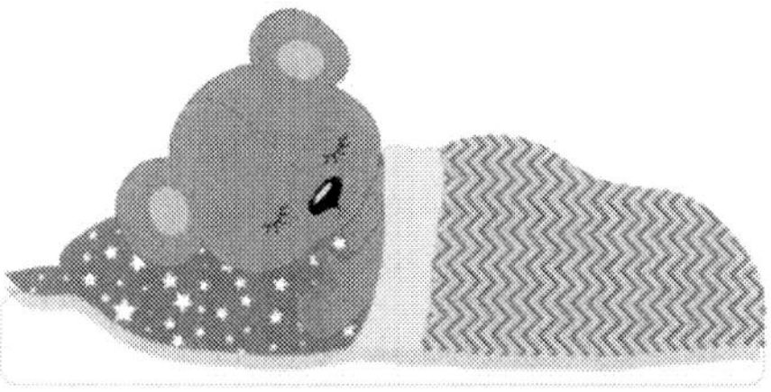

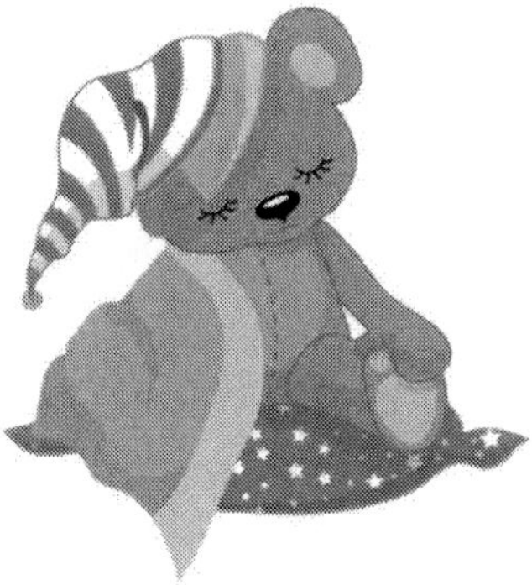

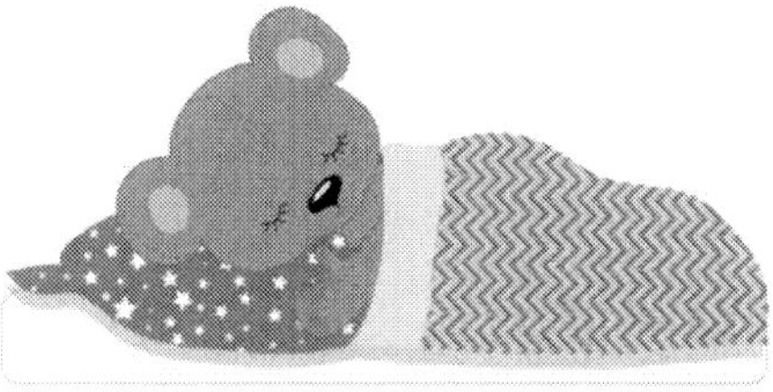

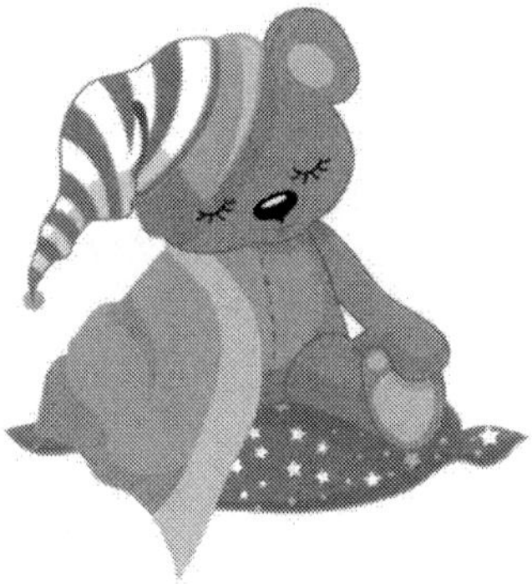

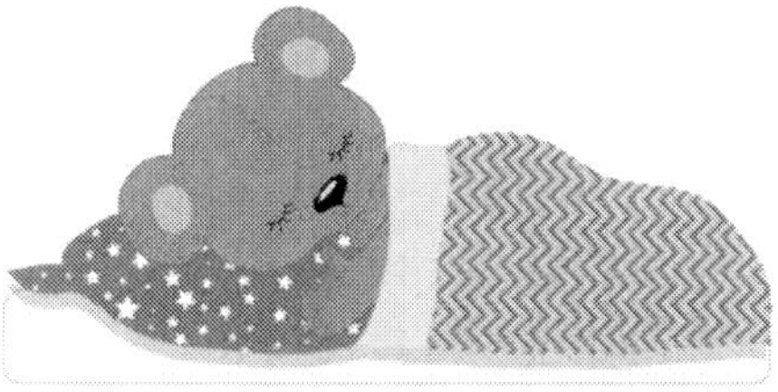

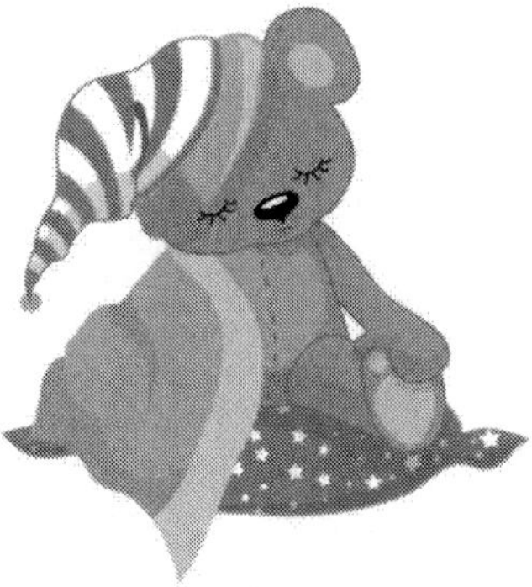

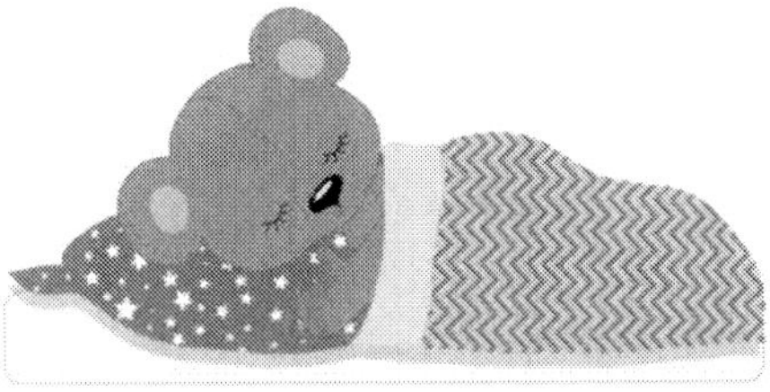

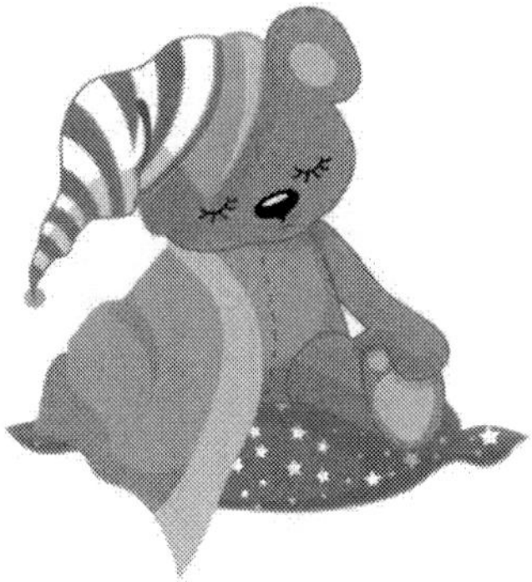

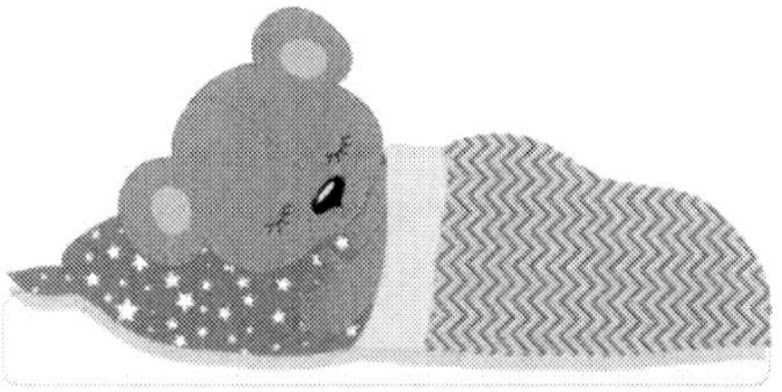

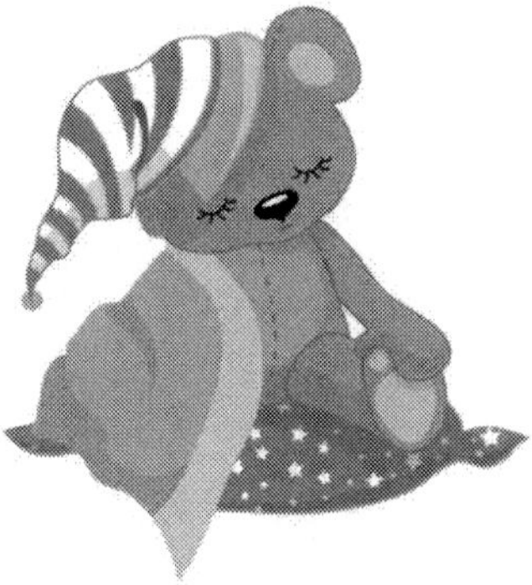

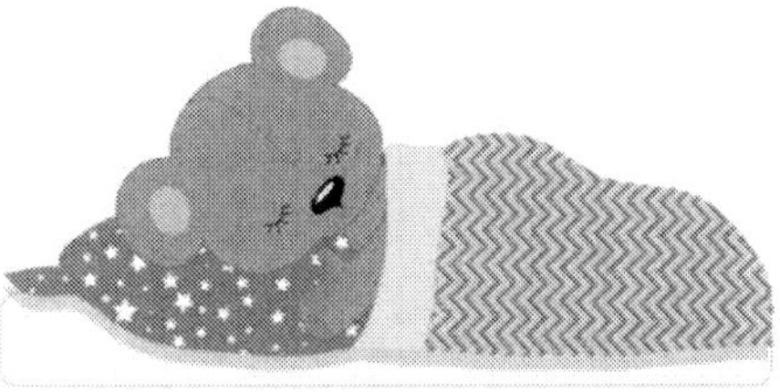

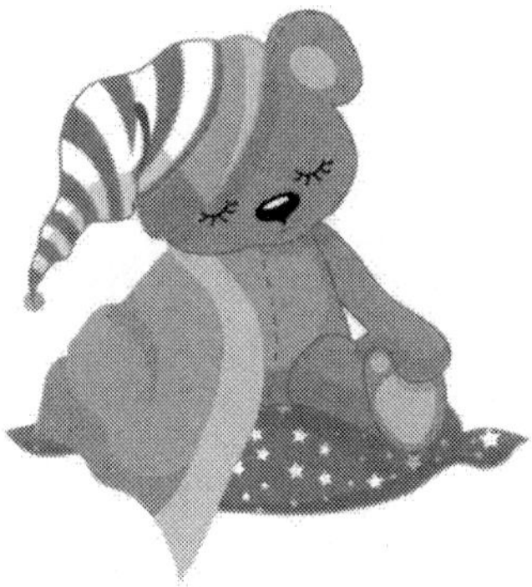

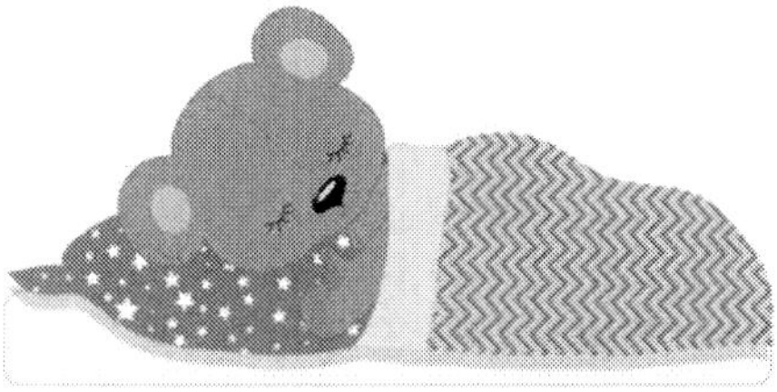

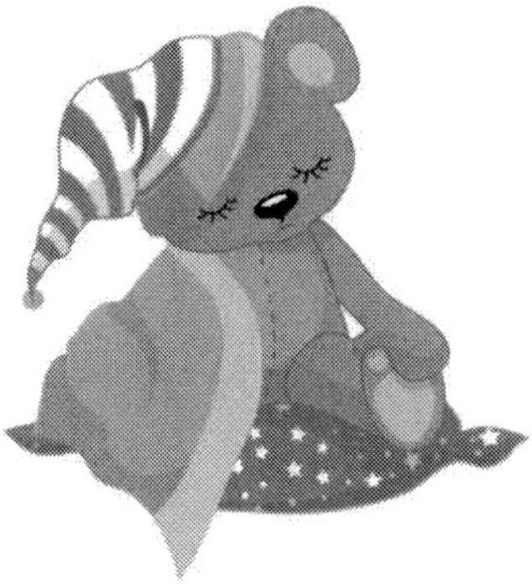

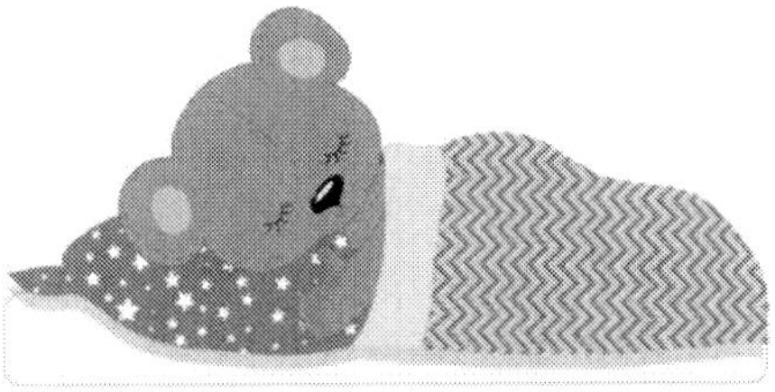

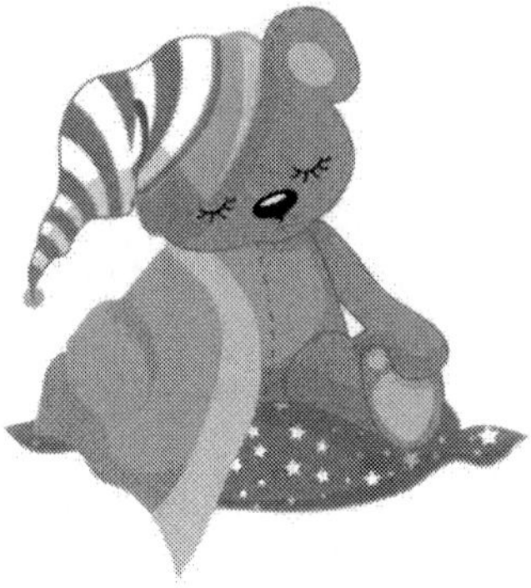

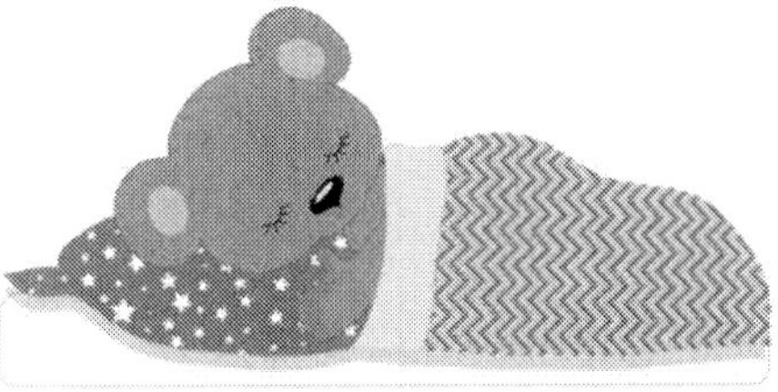

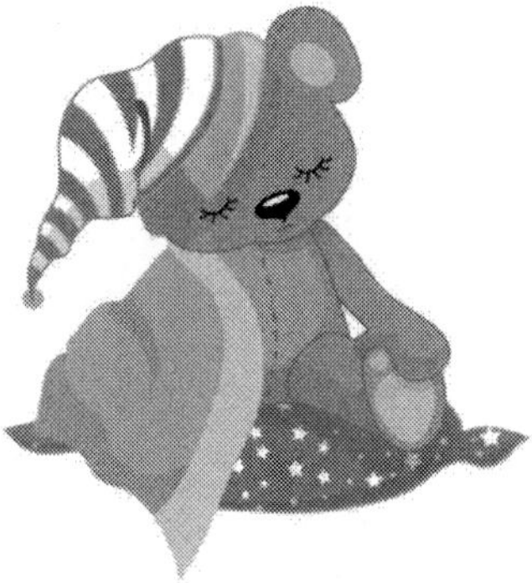

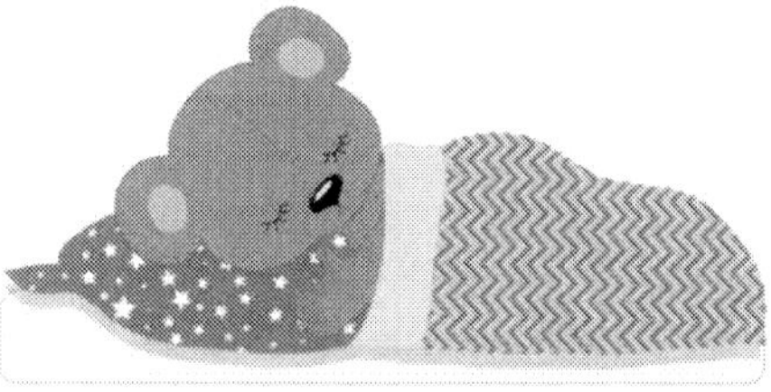

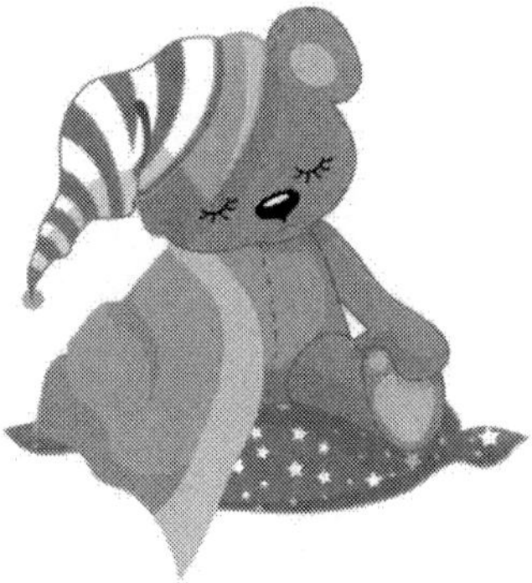

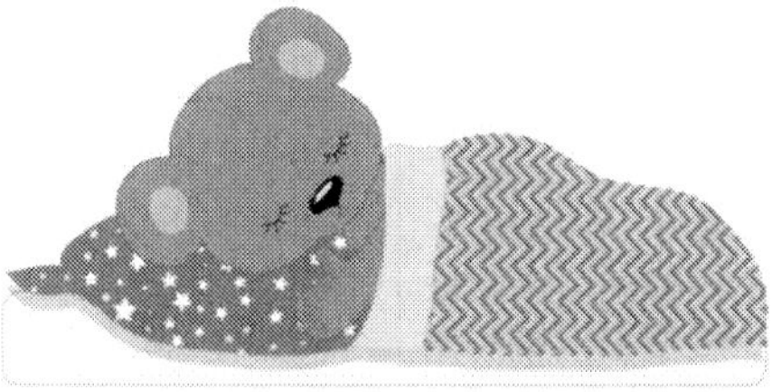

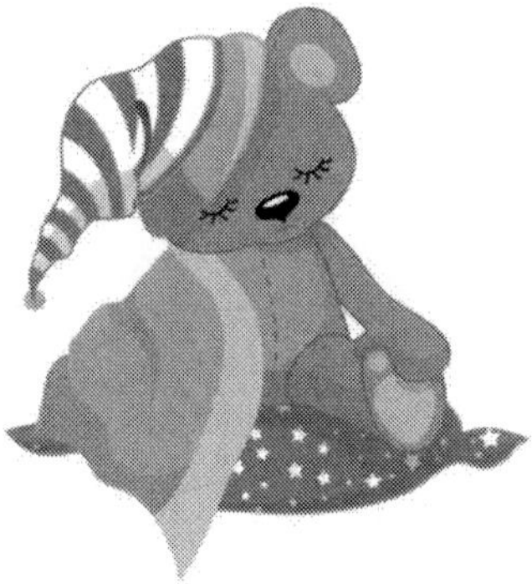

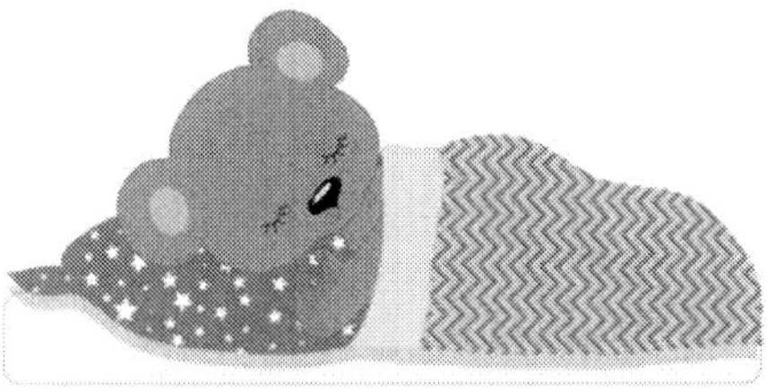

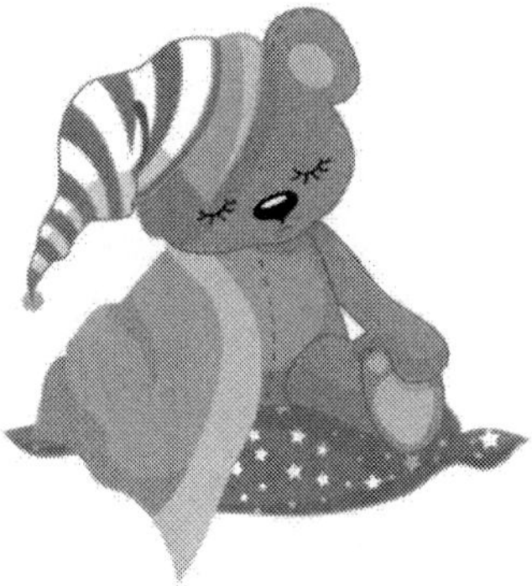

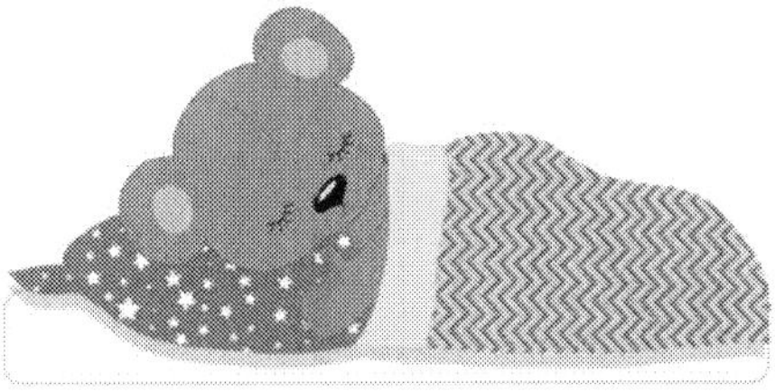

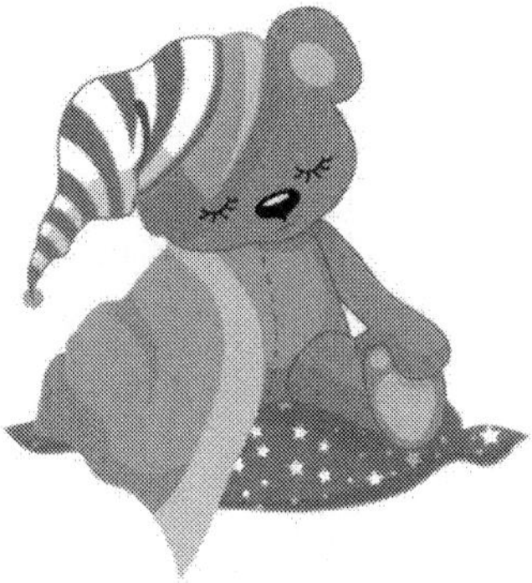

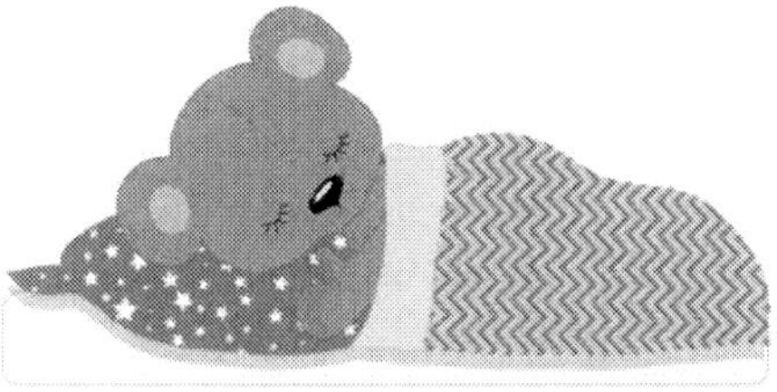

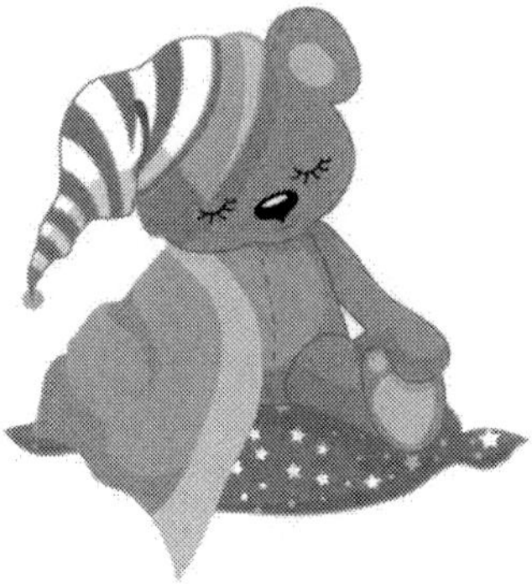

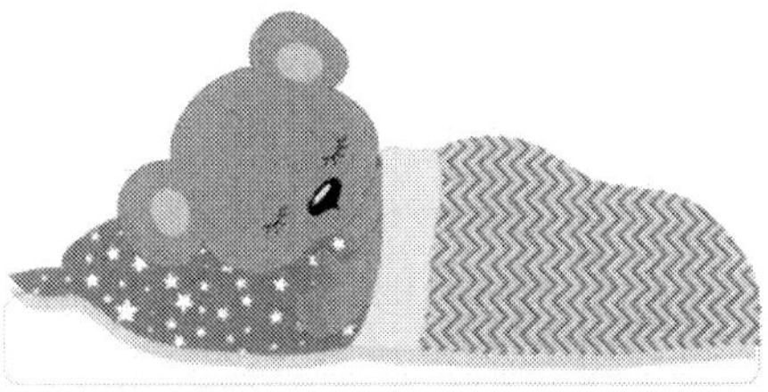

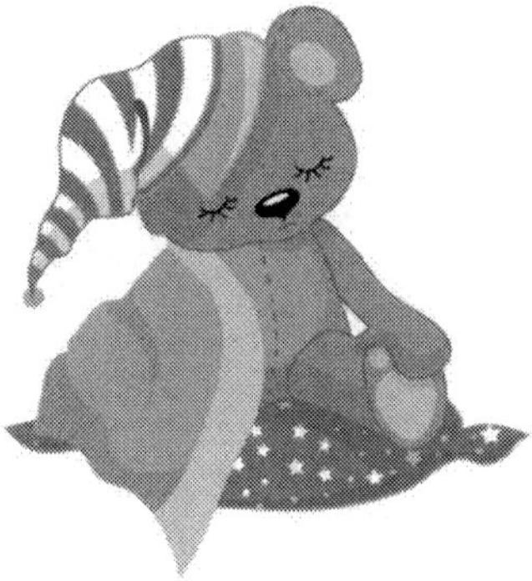

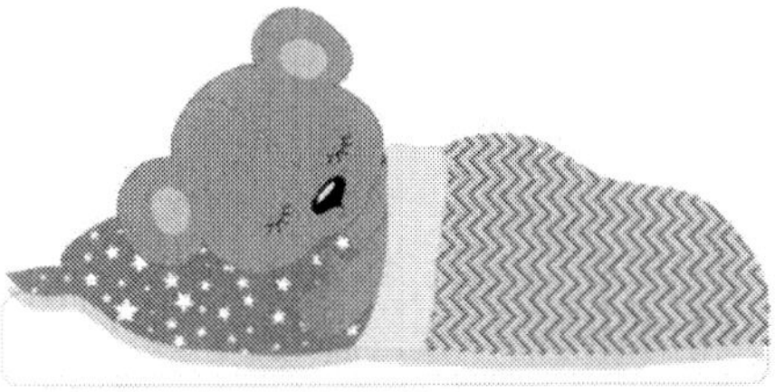

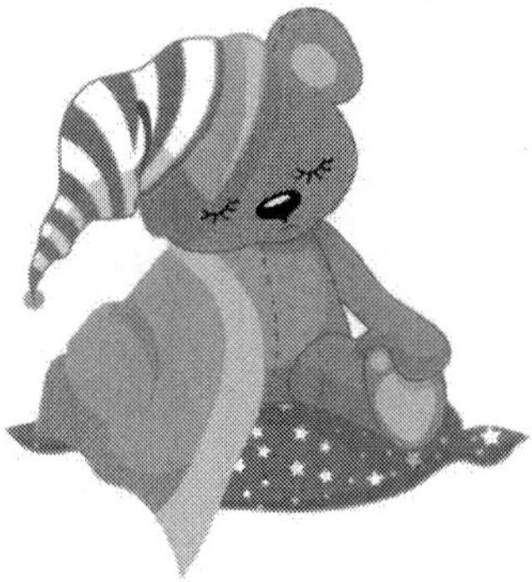

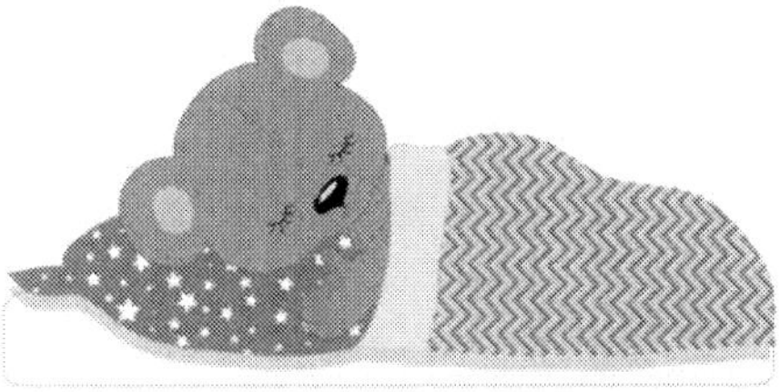

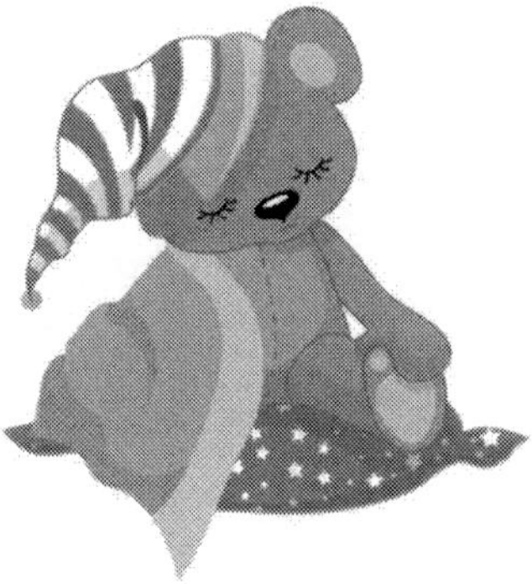

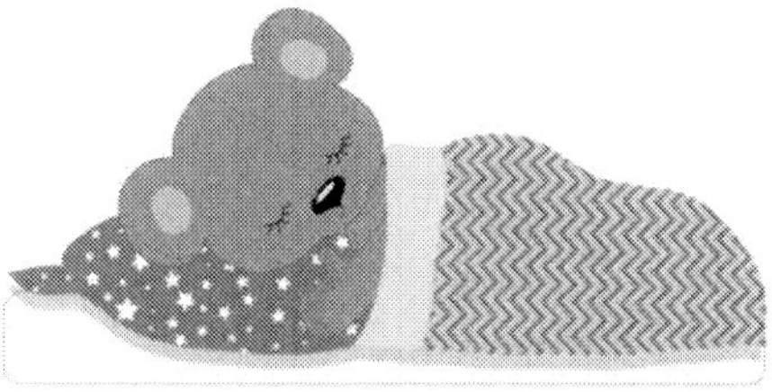

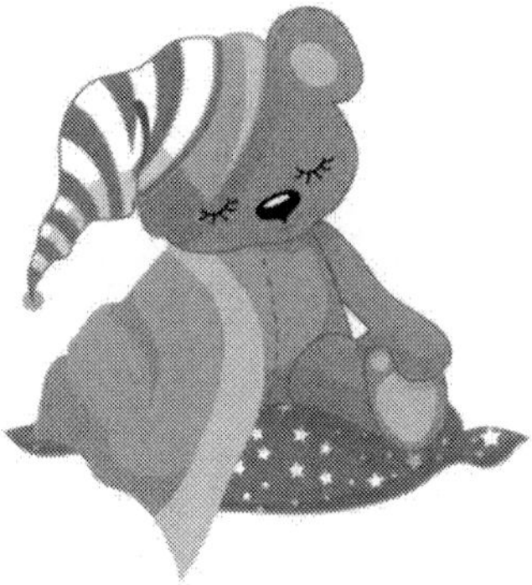

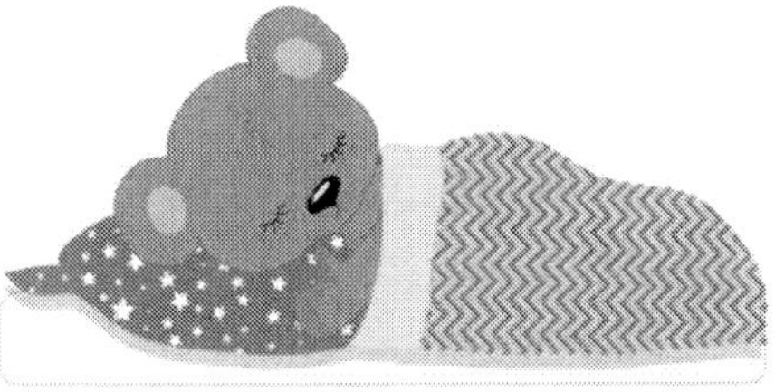

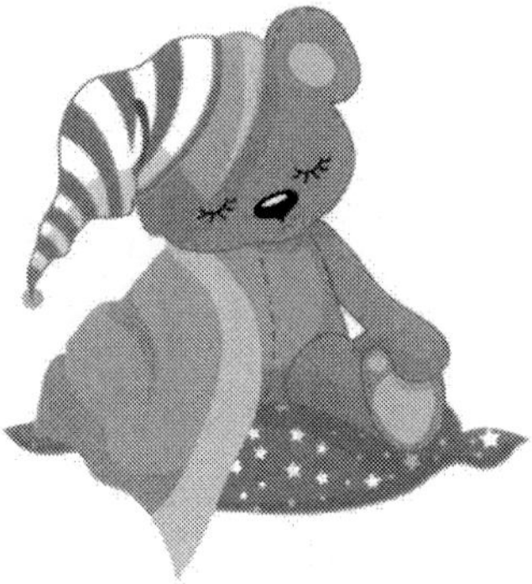

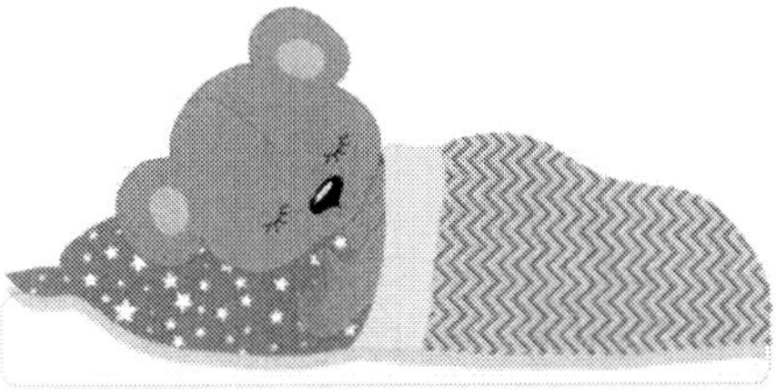

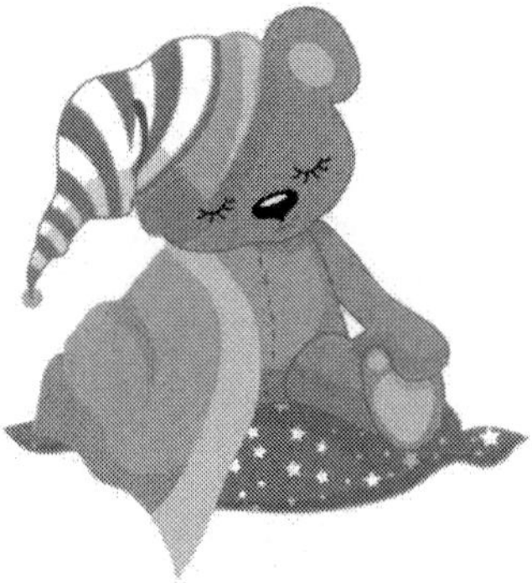

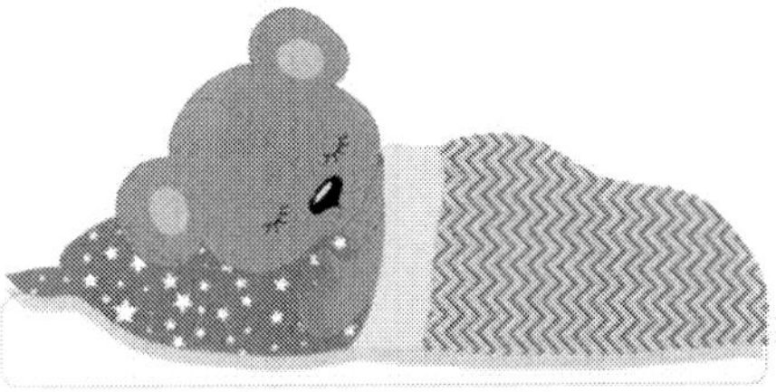

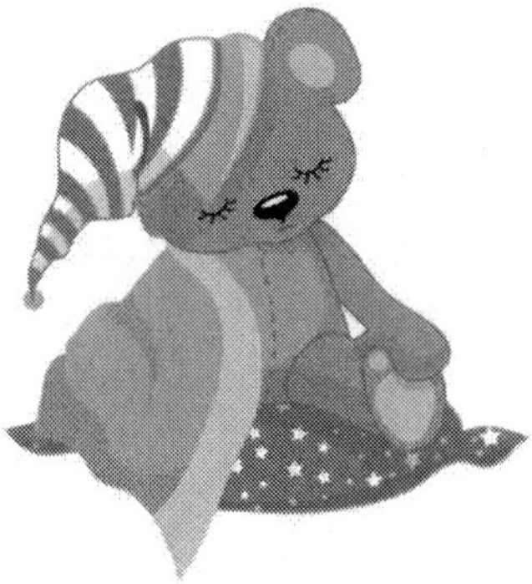

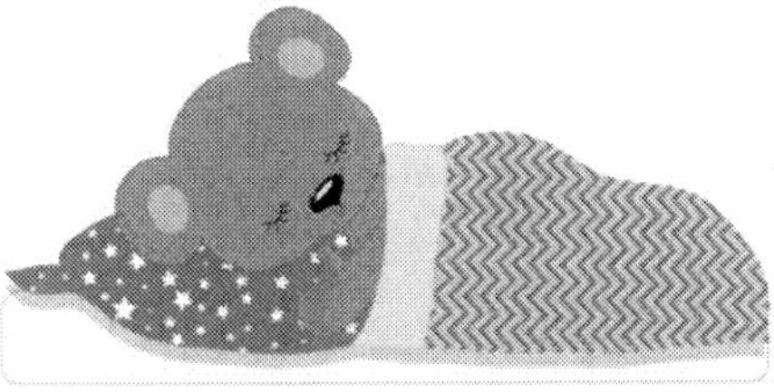

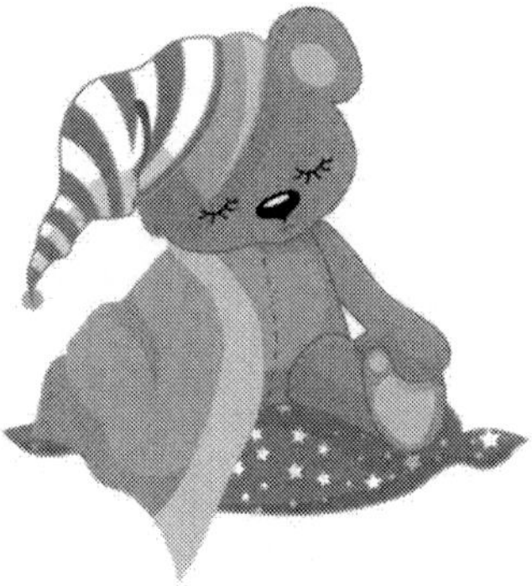

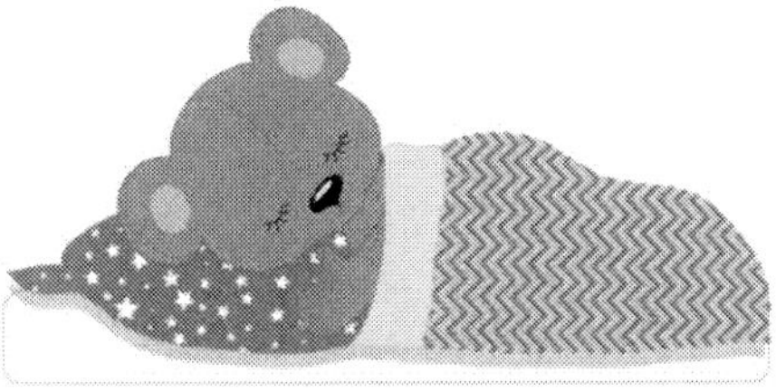

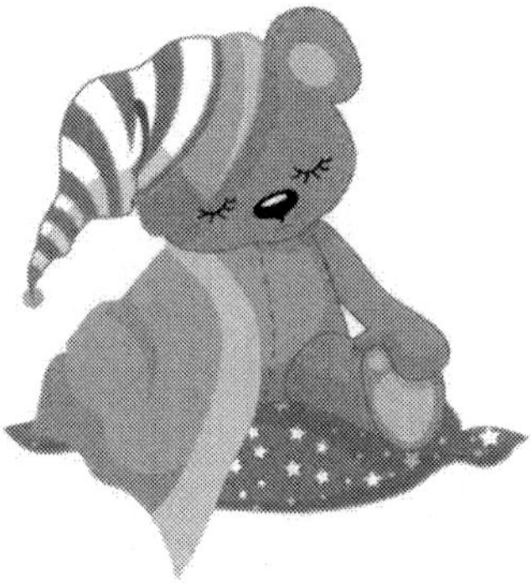

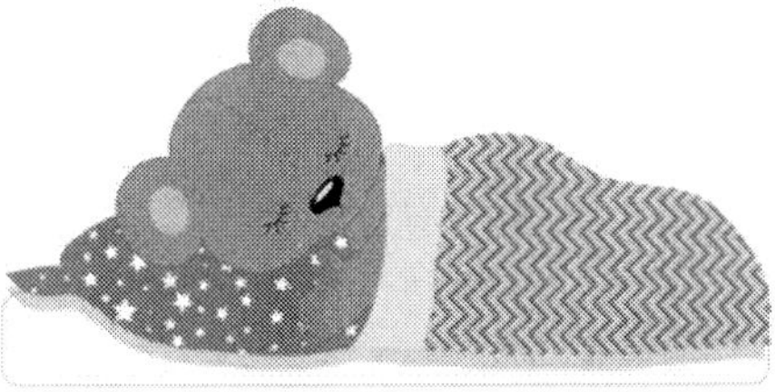

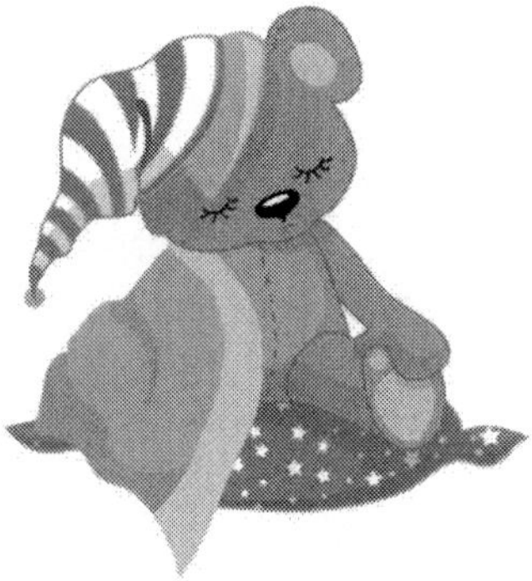

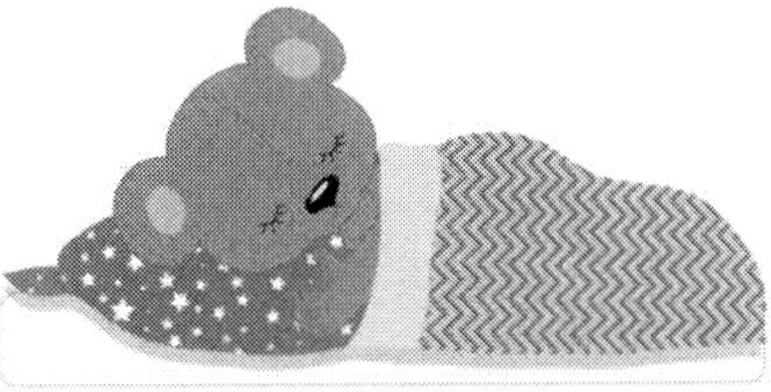

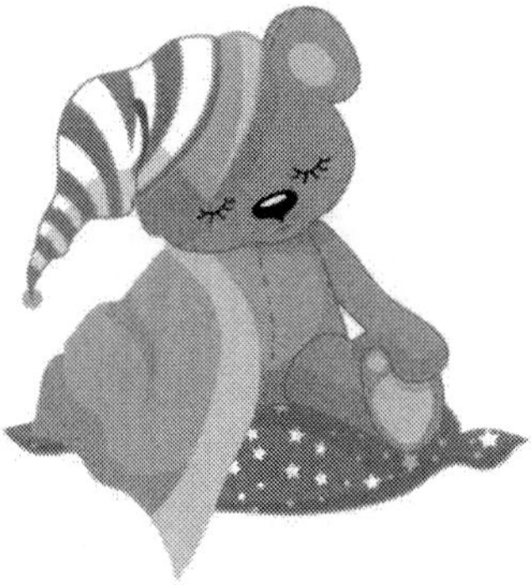

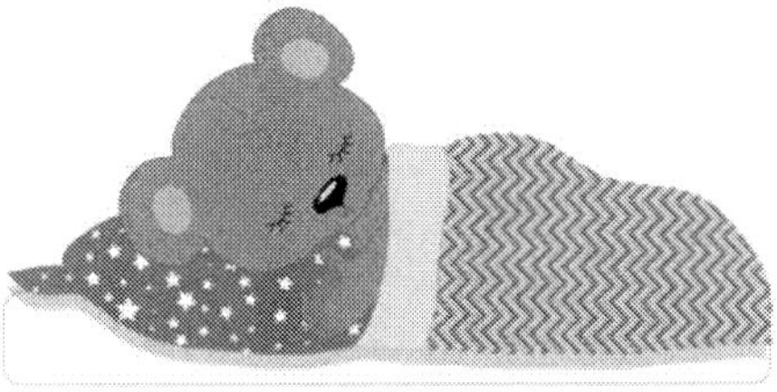

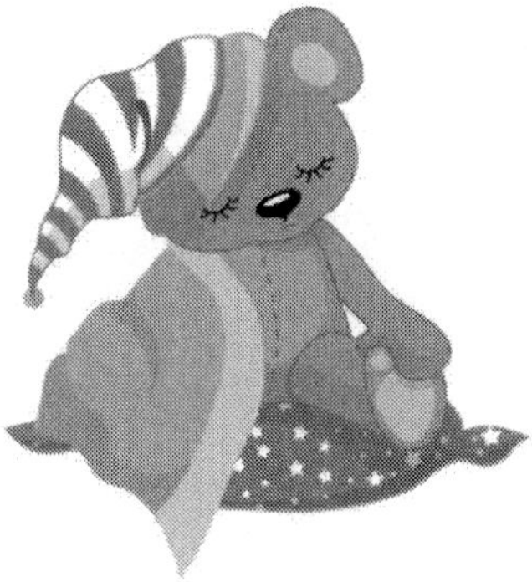

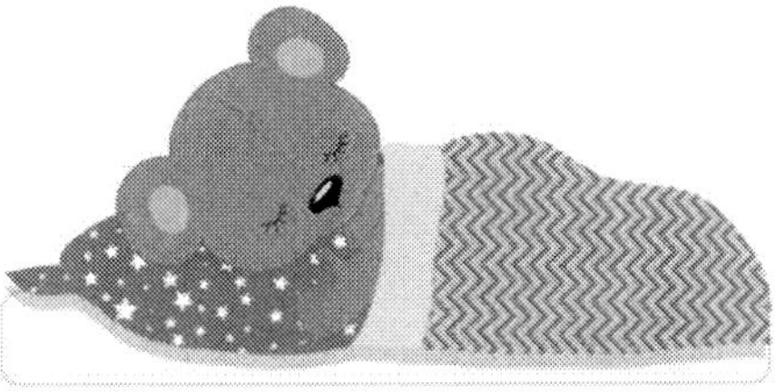

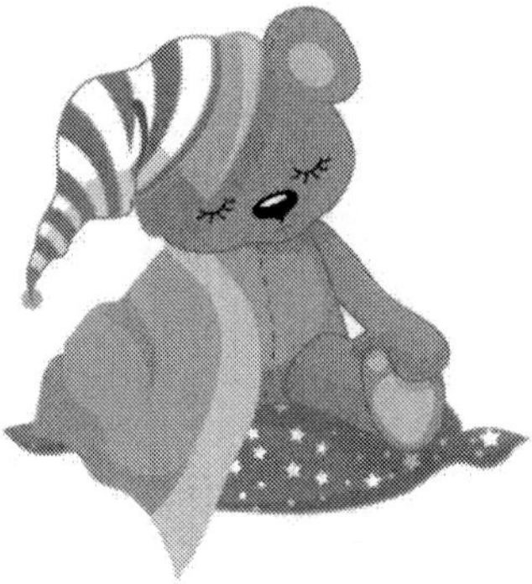

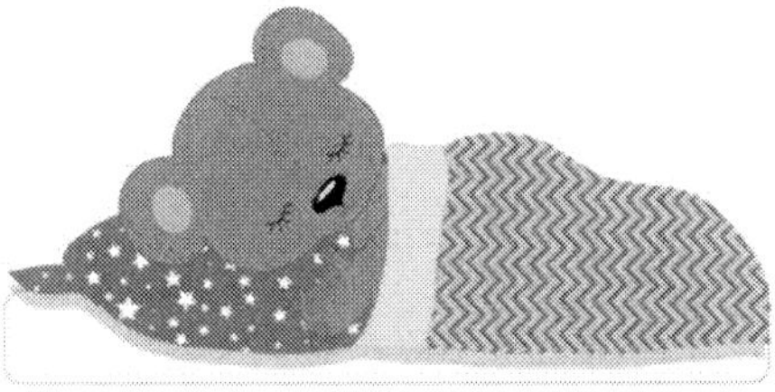

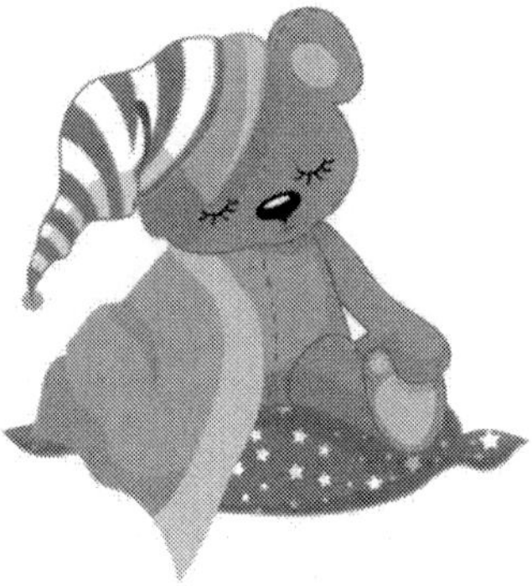

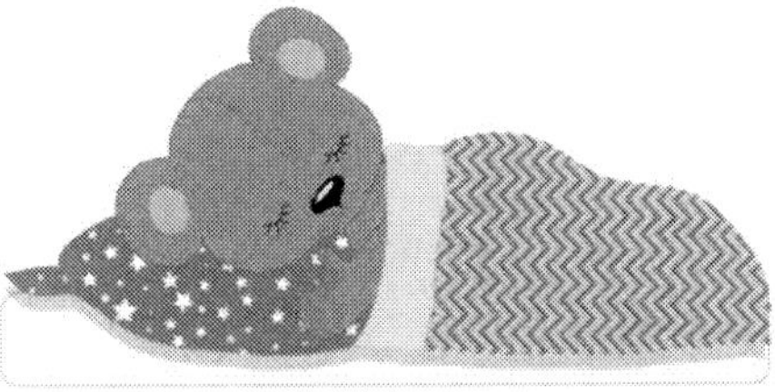

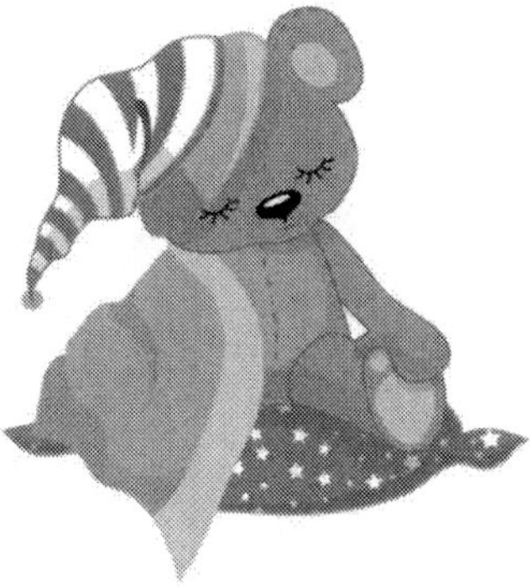

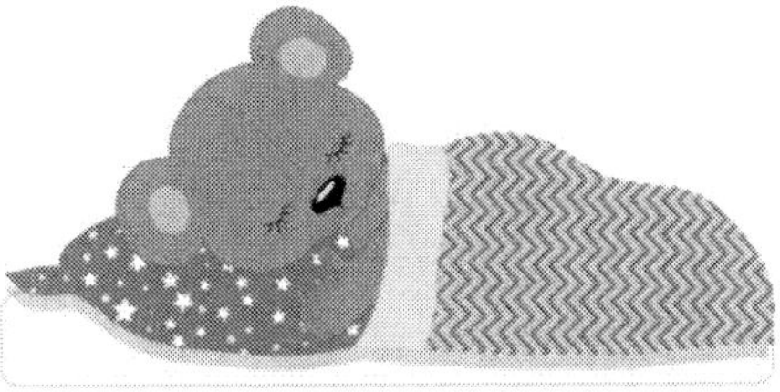

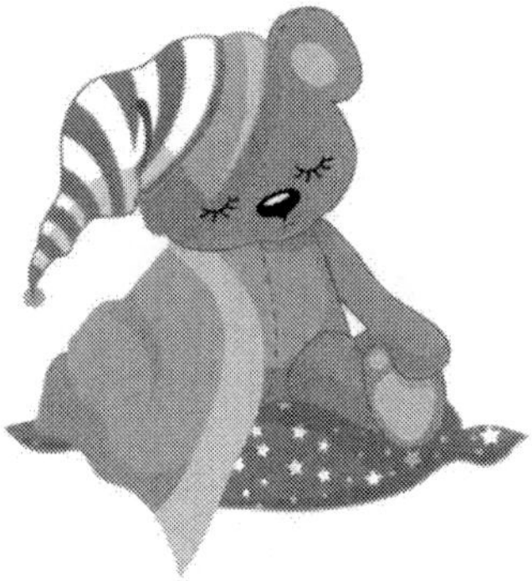

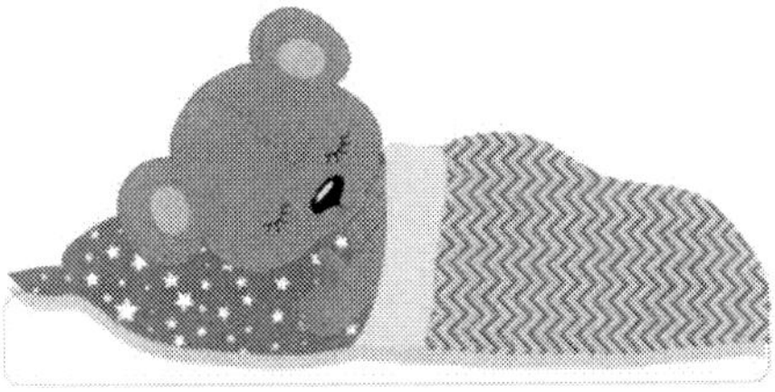

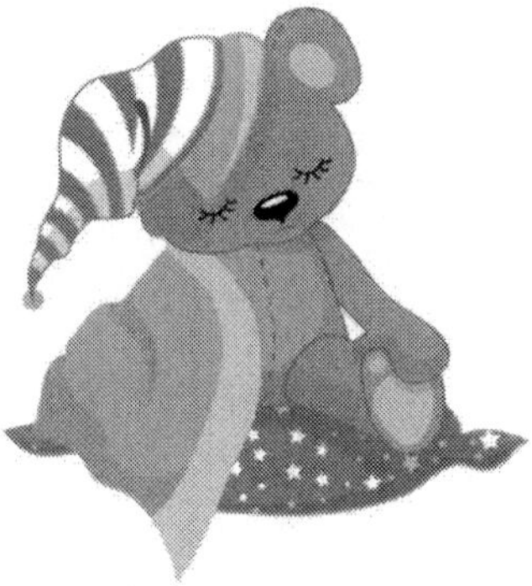

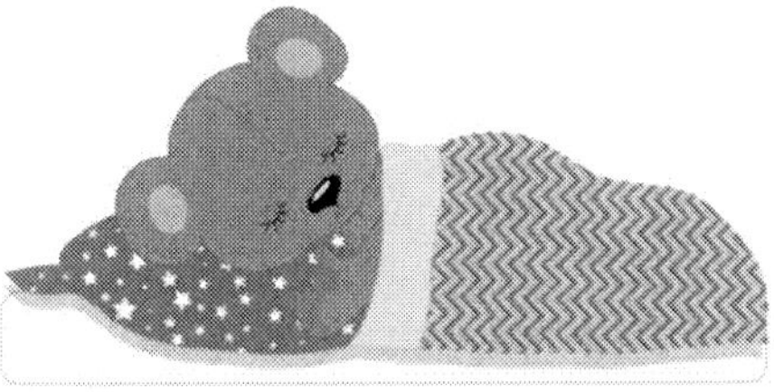

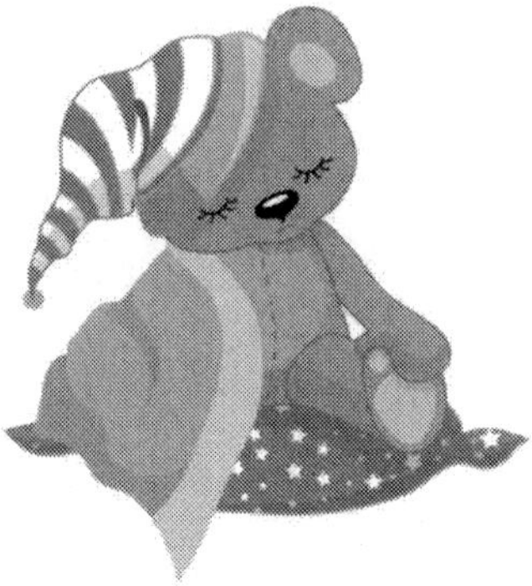

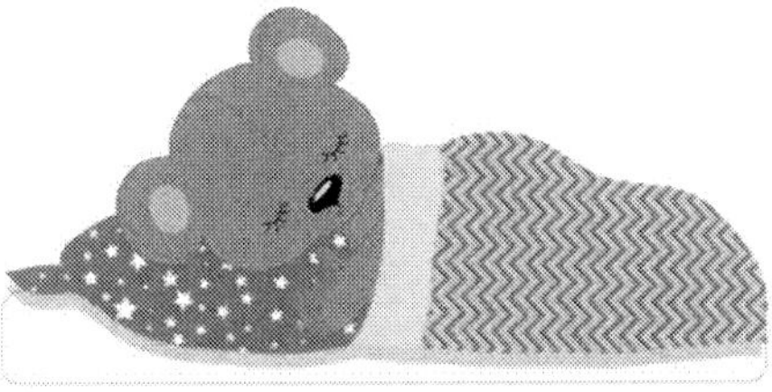

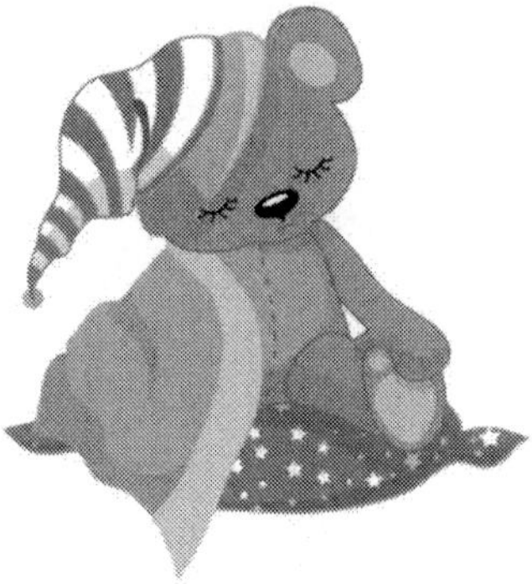

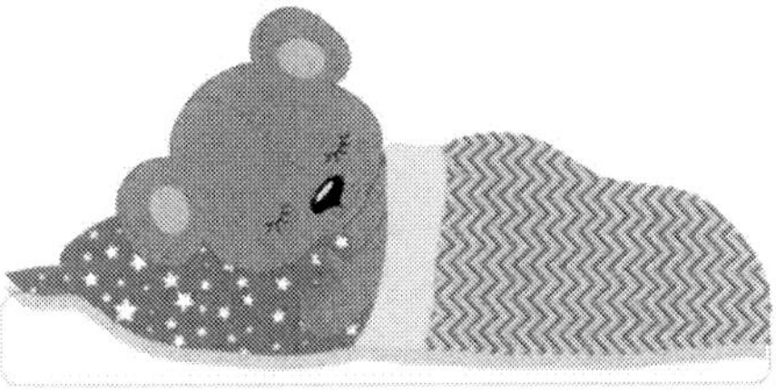

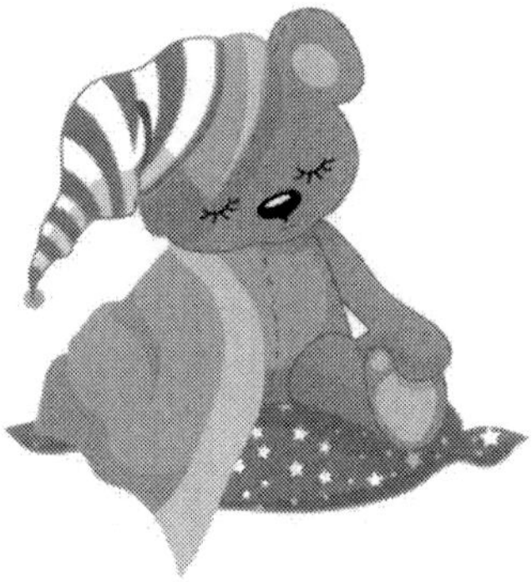

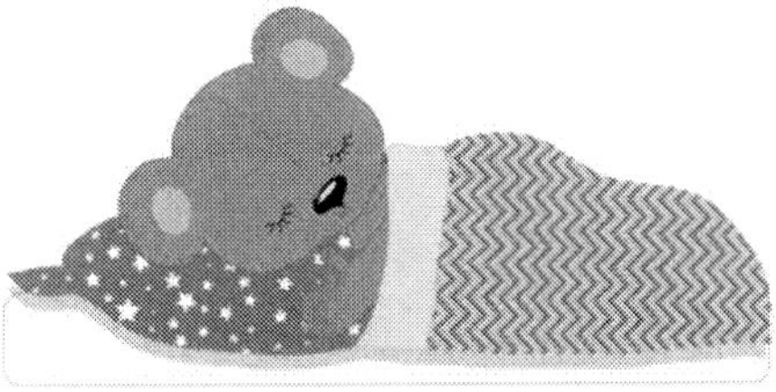

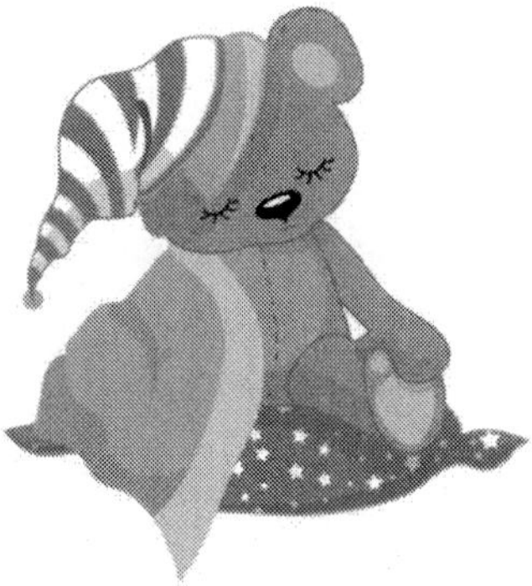

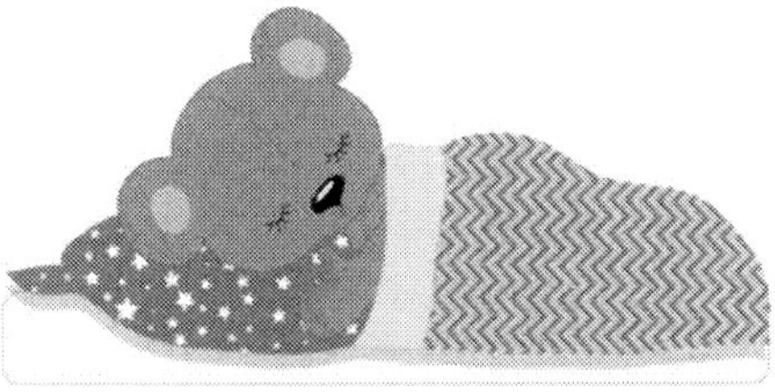

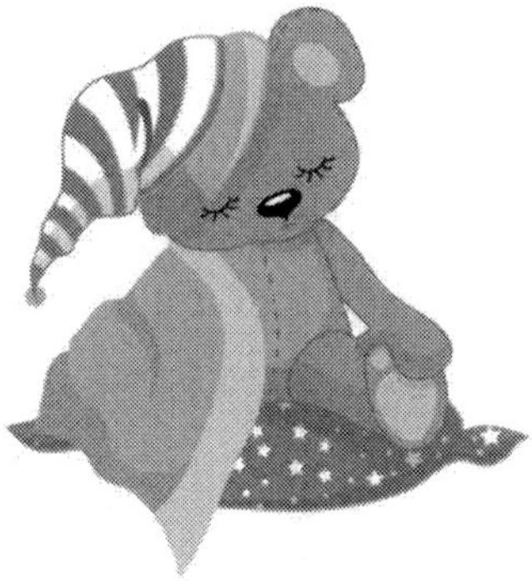

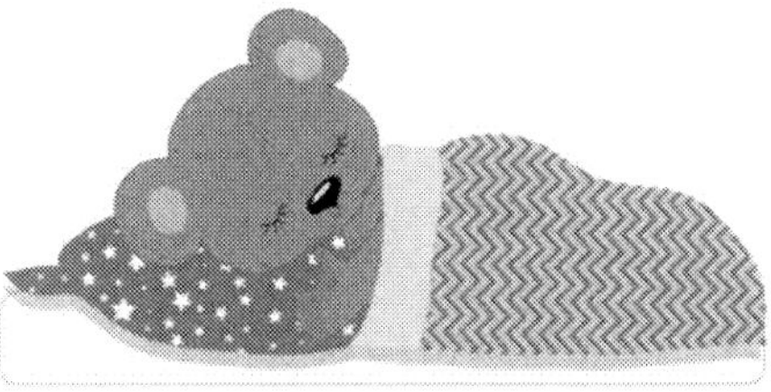

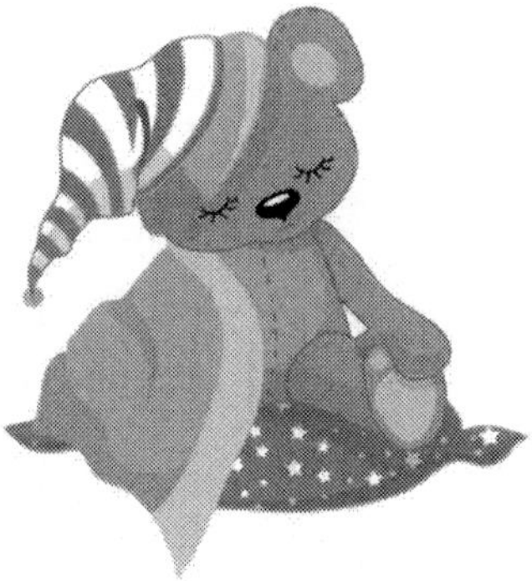

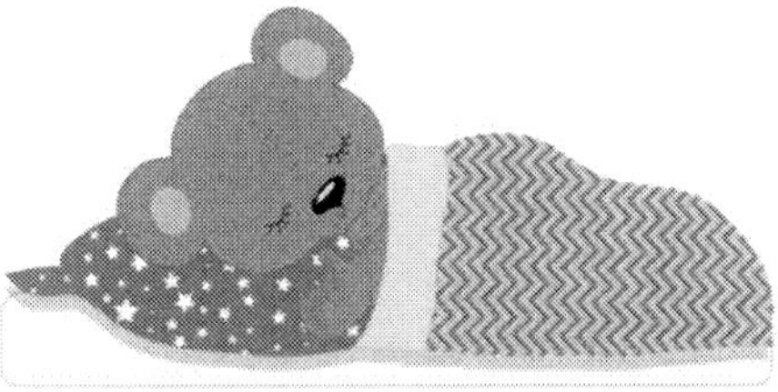

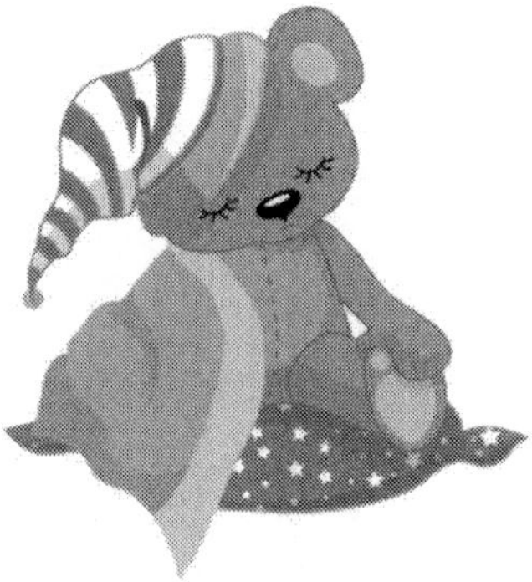

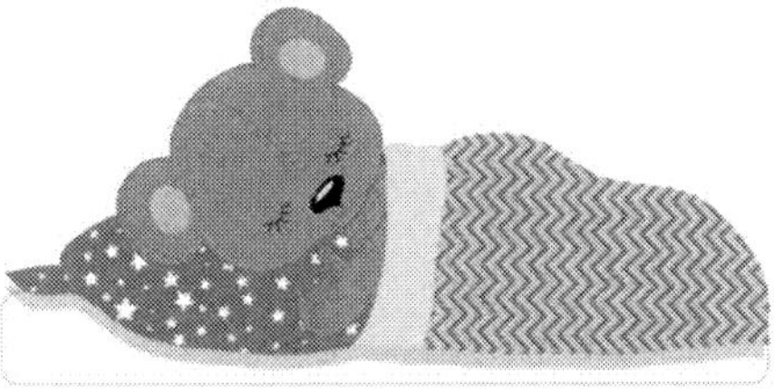

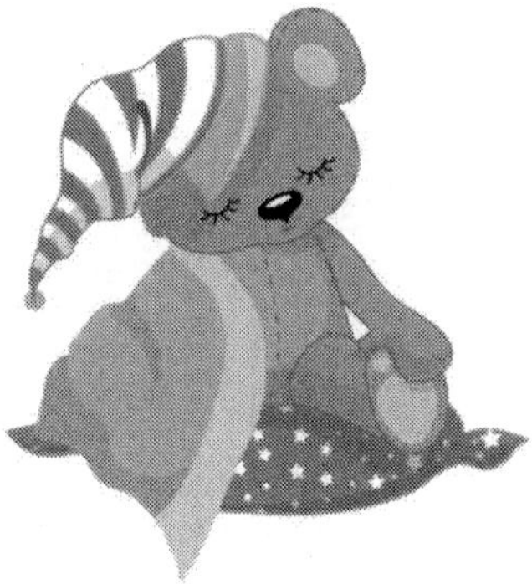

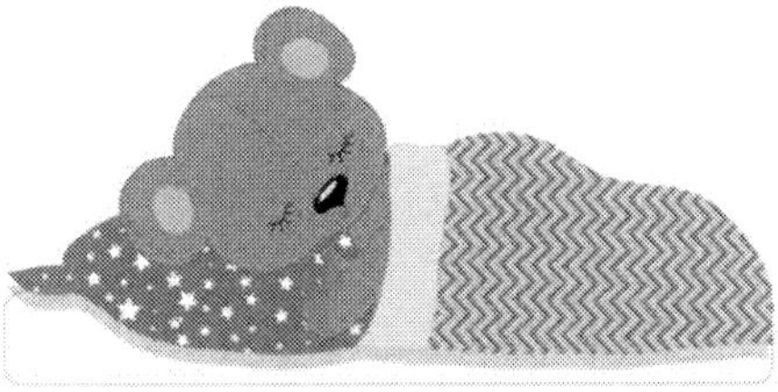

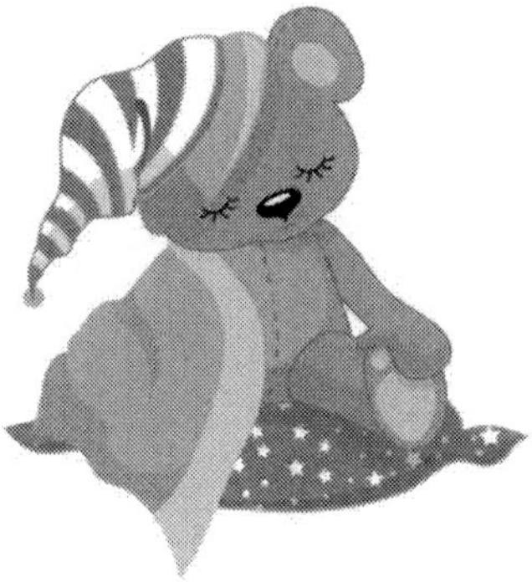

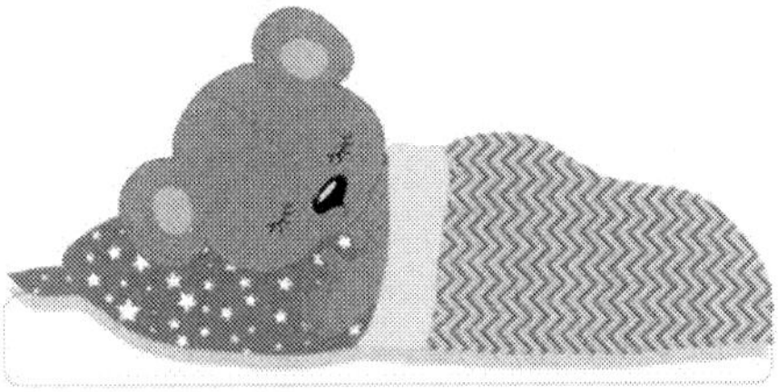

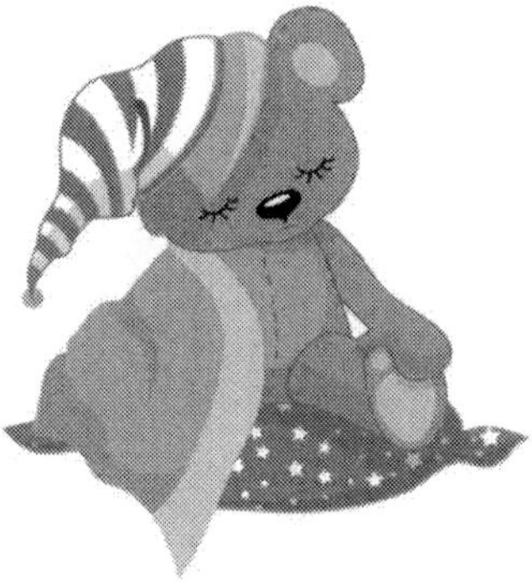

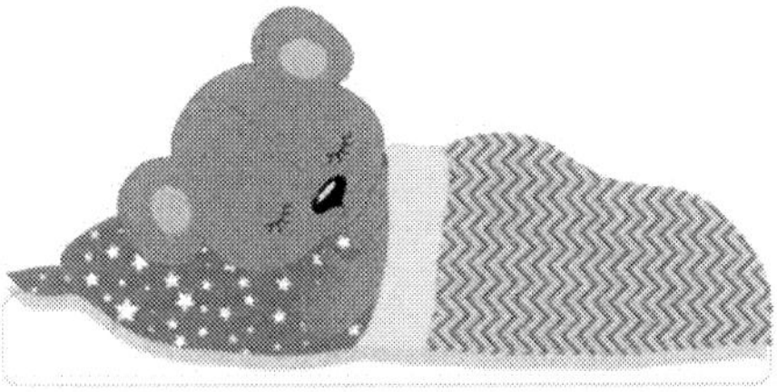

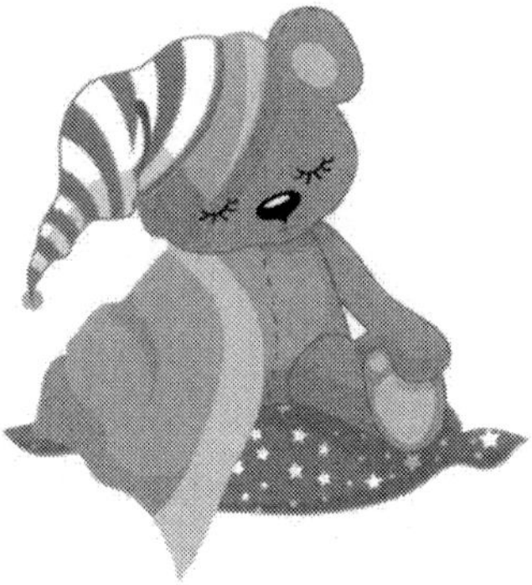

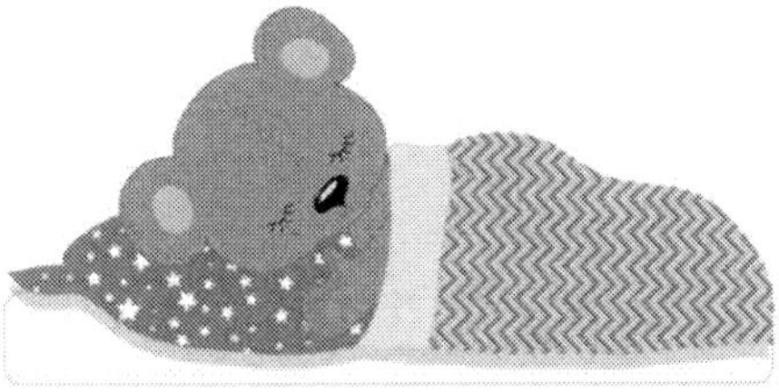

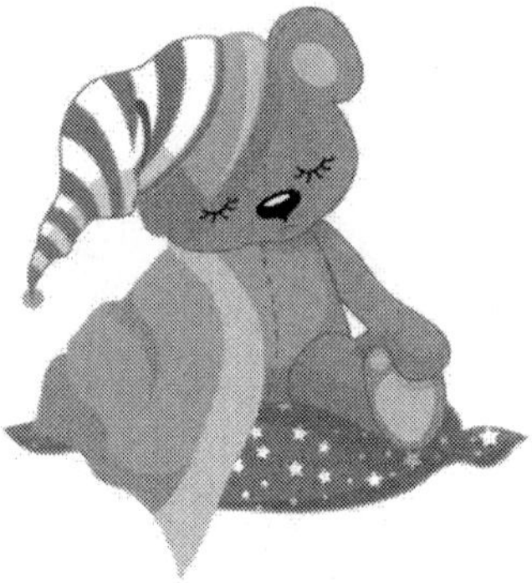

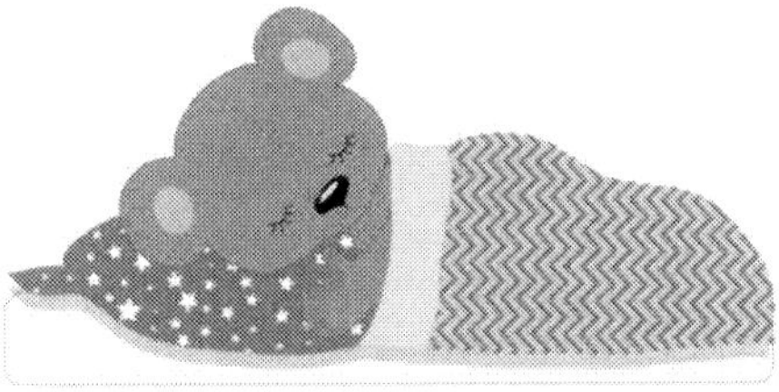

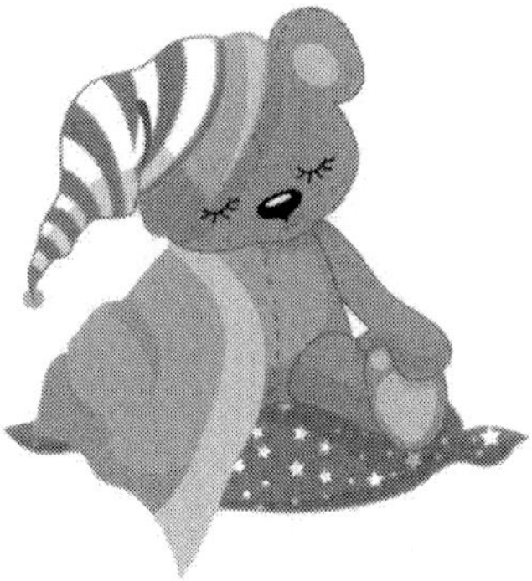

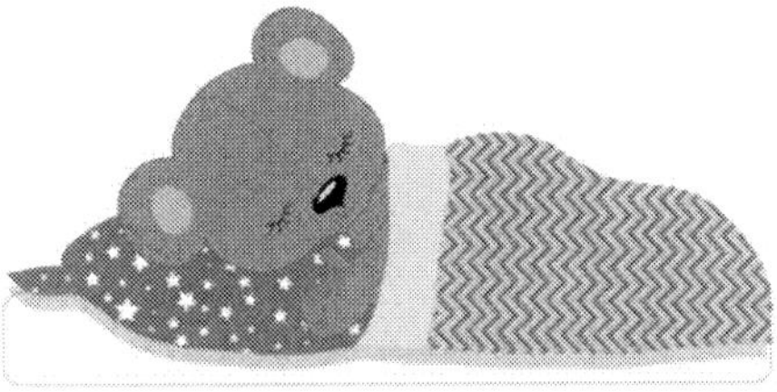

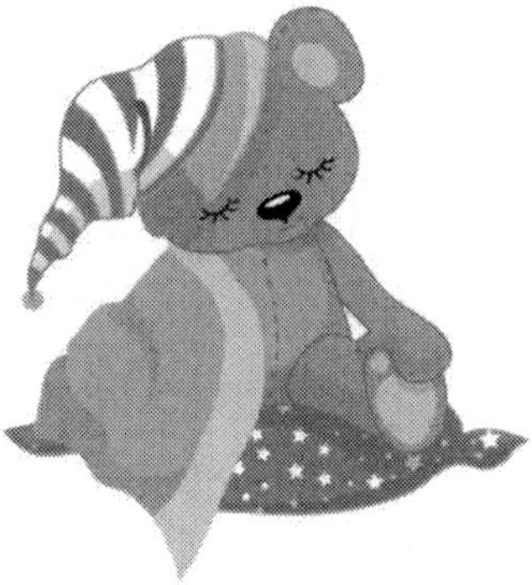

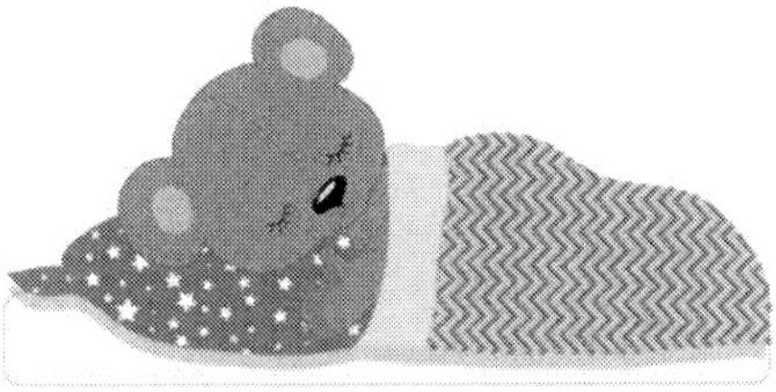

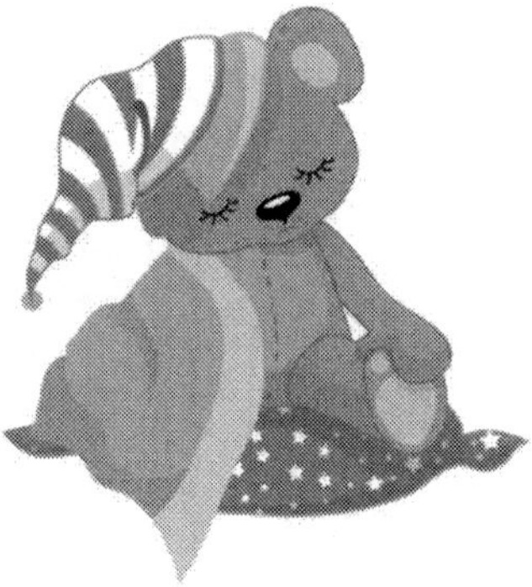

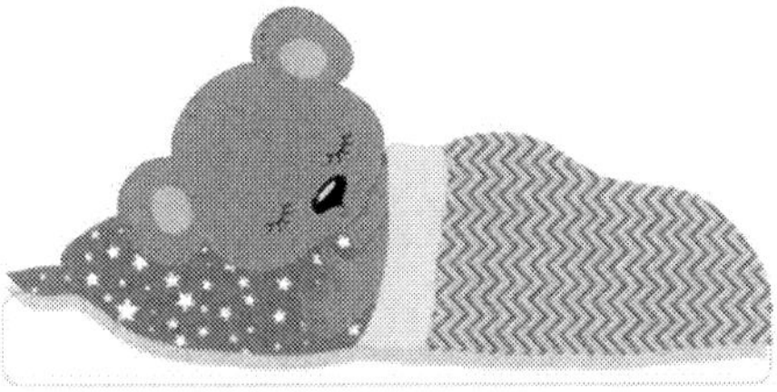

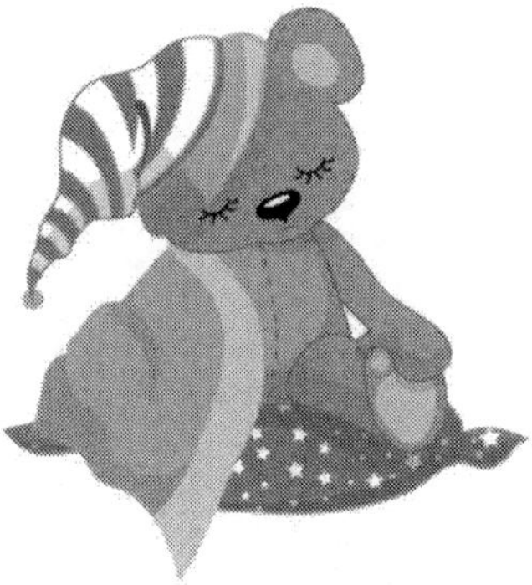

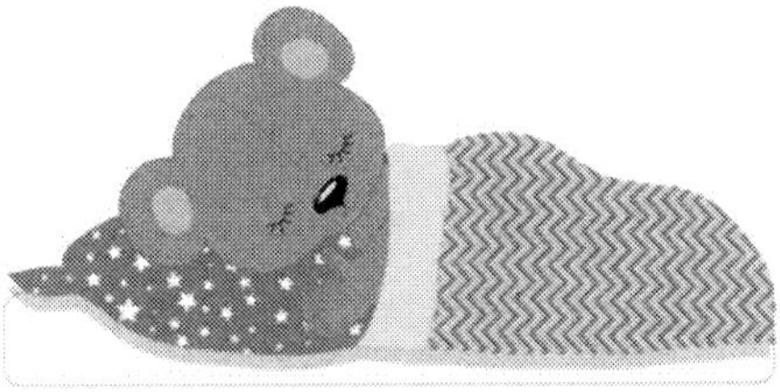

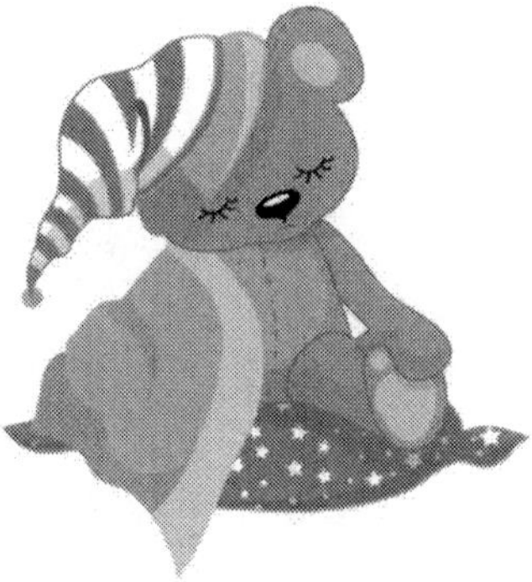

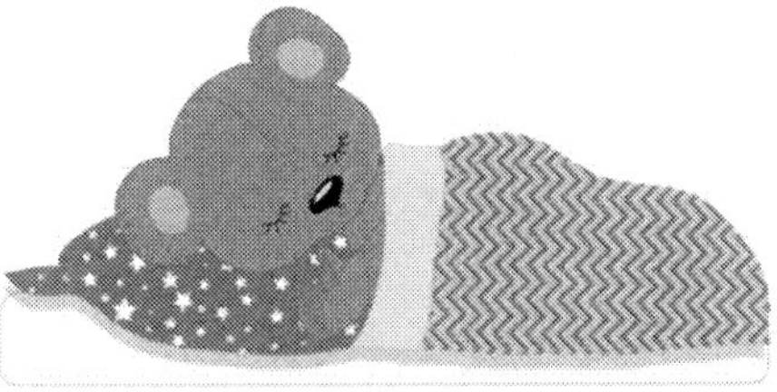

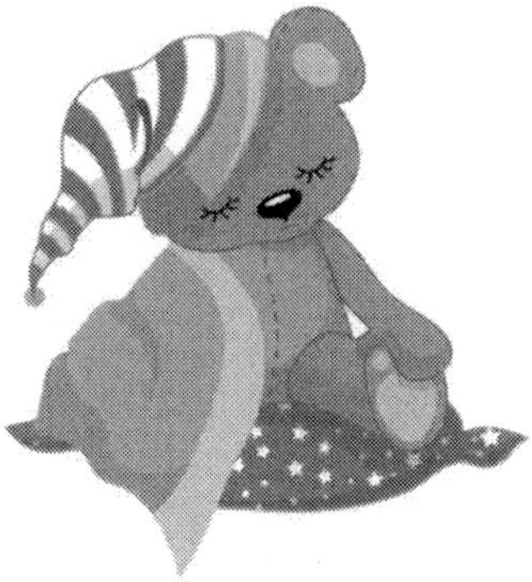

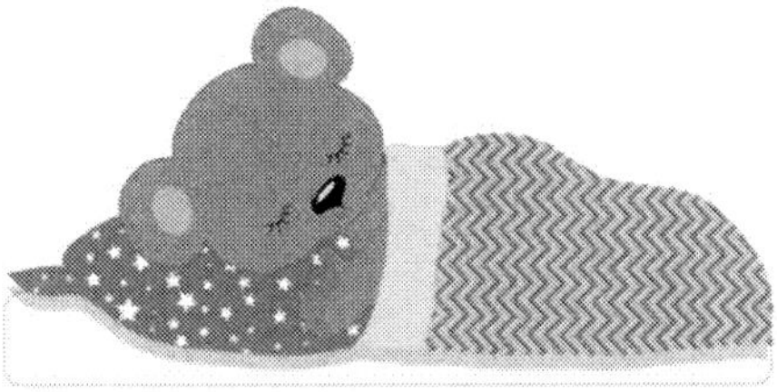

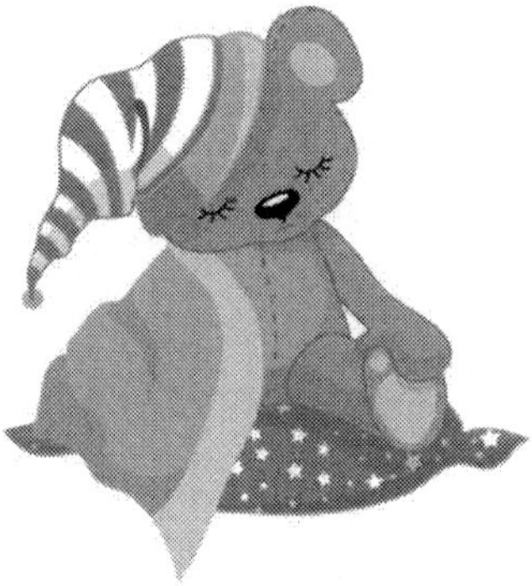

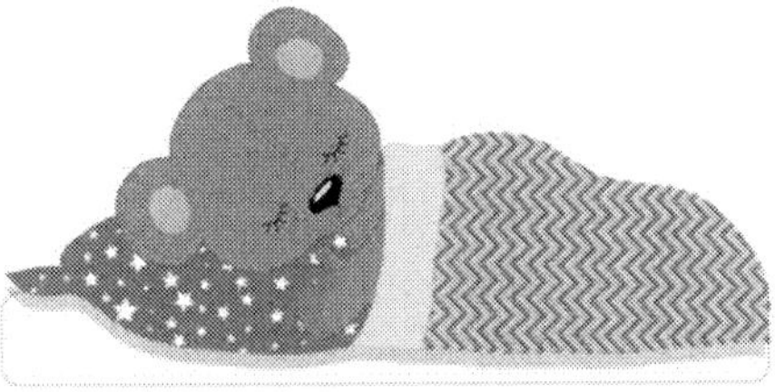

50113654R10069

Made in the USA
San Bernardino, CA
27 August 2019